Pocket
SAN FRANCISCO

TOP SIGHTS · LOCAL LIFE · MADE EASY

Alison Bing

In This Book

QuickStart Guide

Your keys to understanding the city – we help you decide what to do and how to do it

Need to Know
Tips for a smooth trip

Neighborhoods
What's where

Explore San Francisco

The best things to see and do, neighborhood by neighborhood

Top Sights
Make the most of your visit

Local Life
The insider's city

The Best of San Francisco

The city's highlights in handy lists to help you plan

Best Walks
See the city on foot

San Francisco's Best...
The best experiences

Survival Guide

Tips and tricks for a seamless, hassle-free city experience

Getting Around
Travel like a local

Essential Information
Including where to stay

Our selection of the city's best places to eat, drink and experience:

◎ **Sights**

✖ **Eating**

🚻 **Drinking**

✪ **Entertainment**

🔒 **Shopping**

These symbols give you the vital information for each listing:

🕿 Telephone Numbers	👪 Family-Friendly
🕙 Opening Hours	🐾 Pet-Friendly
Ⓟ Parking	🚌 Bus
🚭 Nonsmoking	⛴ Ferry
@ Internet Access	Ⓜ Metro
🛜 Wi-Fi Access	Ⓢ Subway
🌱 Vegetarian Selection	Ⓣ Tram
📖 English-Language Menu	Ⓡ Train

Find each listing quickly on maps for each neighborhood:

Bar Hemingway

16 🚻 Map p233, B2

Legend has it that Hemi self, wielding a machine rate this timber-pan red bar during en by Papa ar town. Dress s.com; Hôtel Rit 🕙 6.30pm-2a

6 ◎ *Plac*

Lonely Planet's San Francisco

Lonely Planet Pocket Guides are designed to get you straight to the heart of the city.

Inside you'll find all the must-see sights, plus tips to make your visit to each one really memorable. We've split the city into easy-to-navigate neighborhoods and provided clear maps so you'll find your way around with ease. Our expert author has searched out the best of the city: walks, food, nightlife and shopping, to name a few. Because you want to explore, our 'Local Life' pages will take you to some of the most exciting areas to experience the real San Francisco.

And of course you'll find all the practical tips you need for a smooth trip: itineraries for short visits, how to get around, and how much to tip the guy who serves you a drink at the end of a long day's exploration.

It's your guarantee of a really great experience.

Our Promise

You can trust our travel information because Lonely Planet authors visit the places we write about, each and every edition. We never accept freebies for positive coverage, so you can rely on us to tell it like it is.

QuickStart Guide 7

Explore San Francisco 21

Worth a Trip:

The Best of San Francisco 161

San Francisco's Best Walks

San Francisco's Best ...

Survival Guide 183

QuickStart Guide

Welcome to San Francisco

Grab your coat and a handful of glitter, and enter the land of fog and fabulousness. If there's a skateboard move yet to be busted, a technology still unimagined, a green scheme untested or quirk left uncelebrated, chances are it's about to happen here. So long, inhibitions; hello, San Francisco.

Downtown vistas from Alamo Square Park (p136)
MARGARETHE WICHERT / GETTY IMAGES ©

👁 San Francisco Top Sights

Golden Gate Bridge (p24)

When afternoon fog rolls in, poof! San Francisco's iconic landmark disappears. Mornings the Golden Gate Bridge reappears, orange against blue skies – a trick assisted by 25 daredevil painters, who apply 1000 gallons of paint weekly.

Alcatraz (p48)

No prisoner escaped this notorious island prison alive – not officially, anyway – but once the door clangs behind you in D-Block solitary, the 1.25-mile swim through riptides seems worth a shot. On the return ferry ride to San Francisco, freedom never felt so good.

JEWHYTE / GETTY IMAGES ©

Exploratorium (p50)

The Exploratorium isn't a museum – it's a total trip, with experiential, psychedelic science exhibits. Enter a colorless world, grope through the pitch-black Tactile Dome, sip glowing cocktails in the Ultraviolet Room and emerge enlightened.

BARRY WINIKER / GETTY IMAGES ©

Golden Gate Park (p144)

San Franciscans have successfully preserved this 1.5-mile wild streak since 1866, ousting casinos, resorts and an igloo village. Today everything San Francisco really needs is here: inspiration, nature and micro-brewed beer at the Beach Chalet.

de Young Museum (p148)

The copper-clad de Young is oxidizing green to match the park, but its eclectic collection is a showstopper. Creative breakthroughs await at every turn: 1980s Keith Haring graffiti, 1960s Oscar de la Renta ball gowns, 1890s Oceanic masks.

Coit Tower & Filbert Street Steps (p54)

Wild parrots may mock your progress up Telegraph Hill's garden-lined Filbert staircase, but they can't keep these bay vistas to themselves. Panoramas and jaw-dropping 1930s murals reward climbs to Coit Tower.

California Academy of Sciences (p146)

Some 40,000 creatures greet your arrival at the Academy. Other museums have galleries – this one has a four-story rainforest, planetarium, aquarium and 60 research scientists working on-site.

Asian Art Museum (p98)

When San Francisco's Pacific Ocean panoramas are lost in fog, you can still see all the way across Asia in this 18,000-piece collection spanning 6000 years, from Pakistan to Japan.

Cable Cars (p76)

Leap onto the baseboard and grab a leather strap – you're in for the ultimate urban carnival ride. When steep climbs yield sudden glimpses of the Golden Gate, public transit never seemed so poetic.

Ferry Building (p74)

The towering achievement here is the sensational, sustainable California bounty that overflows the halls. Award-winning chefs serve signature San Francisco dishes with bay views, and local producers supply constant culinary inspiration.

Marine Life at Fisherman's Wharf (p36)

Sea lions are living the California dream at Pier 39: lolling on docks and feasting on seafood. On the other side of Pier 39, sharks circle at Aquarium of the Bay, separated from visitors by a glass tube.

San Francisco Local Life

Insider tips to help you find the real city

The city with its head perpetually in the clouds is also surprisingly down-to-earth. Dive into San Francisco's neighborhoods to observe its outlandish ideas in action, from graffiti-art-gallery alleyways to certified green saloons.

The History-Making Castro (p130)

▶ Gay history landmarks
▶ LGBT community organizations

The center of the gay world throws the ultimate Pride party – but the Castro's historic triumphs in civil rights, free speech and HIV/AIDS treatment were hard-won. America's first LGBT history museum tells the epic story, and you can join the next chapter now unfolding at Castro community institutions.

Sunny Mission Stroll (p114)

▶ Slacker hotspots
▶ Mural-lined alleyways

Blame it on San Francisco's microclimates: when mists roll over Golden Gate Park, it's still sunny in the Mission. Ditch SF's clammy coast and join the tanning and slacking already in progress – eat organic ice cream on Dolores Park's scenic slope, witness murals and gardens in progress in alleyways, and people-watch on Valencia St over scandalously early happy hours.

Russian Hill & Nob Hill Secrets (p70)

▶ Stairway walks
▶ Inspiration points

High on Russian Hill, find the sources of San Francisco's inspiration: hilltop gardens that practically write their own poetry, hidden stairway walks that inspire best-selling mysteries, and the alley where Jack Kerouac found his mojo and banged out *On the Road* in 20 days. On Nob Hill, state secrets and the mysteries of the universe are revealed – though the Tonga Room's indoor monsoons only make sense to Scorpion Bowl drinkers.

Dolores Park (p115)

Castro Theatre (p131)

Other great places to experience the city like a local:

JE.JIN / GETTY IMAGES ©

BUYENLARGE / GETTY IMAGES ©

San Francisco Day Planner

Day One

☀ Leap onto the Powell-Mason cable car: you're in for hills and thrills. Hop off in North Beach and hike to **Coit Tower** (p54) for groundbreaking murals and giddy, 360-degree panoramas. Take scenic **Filbert St Steps** (p55) to the sunny Embarcadero waterfront, then plunge into the total darkness of the Tactile Dome inside the **Exploratorium** (p50).

☀ Grab **Mijita's** (p75) sensational fish tacos at the **Ferry Building** (p74), then catch your prebooked ferry to **Alcatraz** (p48). Here escape attempts might have landed you in solitary, and mentions of kisses were censored in library books. Make your island prison break and head to North Beach, where you can read freely at free-speech landmark **City Lights** (p58) and mingle with San Francisco's freest spirits at the **Beat Museum** (p58).

☾ Alcatraz inmates had 20 minutes for dinner – but with reservations, you can linger over North Beach's best pasta at **Cotogna** (p60). Since you just escaped prison, you're tough enough to handle too-close-for-comfort comics at **Cobb's Comedy Club** (p66), or drag satire at **Beach Blanket Babylon** (p66). Toast your day of living dangerously in San Francisco with spur-rattling Pisco sours at **Comstock Saloon** (p64).

Day Two

☀ Hop the N Judah streetcar to **Golden Gate Park** (p144) while carnivorous plants are still enjoying insect breakfasts at **Conservatory of Flowers** (p152). Follow Andy Goldsworthy's artful sidewalk fault lines into the **de Young Museum** (p148), and discover blockbuster basement art shows and faultless tower-top views. Take a walk on the wild side at the **California Academy of Sciences** (p146), where blue butterflies flirt shamelessly with Rainforest Dome visitors. Enjoy a moment of Zen with tea at the **Japanese Tea Garden** (p153) and bliss out in the secret redwood grove at the **San Francisco Botanical Garden** (p152).

☀ Join surfers at **Outerlands** (p154) for artisan grilled cheese and organic soup, then beachcomb **Ocean Beach** (p152) to the **Beach Chalet** (p155) to glimpse 1930s WPA murals celebrating San Francisco. Follow the **Coastal Trail** (p154) past Sutro Baths and Land's End, and watch fog tumble over **Golden Gate Bridge** (p24) and Impressionist dancers twirl at the **Legion of Honor** (p152).

☾ Satisfy cross-cultural cravings with organic Cal-Moroccan feasts at **Aziza** (p153), then stomp to bluegrass at the **Plough & the Stars** (p157).

Short on time?

We've arranged San Francisco's must-sees into these day-by-day itineraries to make sure you see the very best of the city in the time you have available.

Day Three

☀ Take the California St cable car to pagoda-topped Grant St for two Chinatown immersion experiences: **Red Blossom** (p65) tea tastings and **Chinese Historical Society of America** (p58) ephemera collections. Stop by the 1906-fire-scarred altar at **Tin How Temple** (p59) for good luck, then find your fortune at **Golden Gate Fortune Cookie Company** (p68).

☼ Hail dim sum carts for dumplings at **City View** (p62), then head uphill past Commercial St's former Gold Rush 'parlor houses' (read: brothels) to catch the Powell-Hyde cable car. Past zig-zagging **Lombard Street** (p41) you'll reach **Maritime Museum** (p41), where 1930s mosaics reveal underwater worlds. Save the planet from Space Invaders at **Musée Mécanique** (p37), or enter underwater stealth mode inside a real WWII submarine: **USS Pampanito** (p37).

☾ Watch sea lions cavort as the sun fades over **Pier 39** (p37), then hop the F-line streetcar for Nor-Cal fare at **Rich Table** (p103). Browse Hayes Valley boutiques before your **San Francisco Symphony** (p107) or **SFJAZZ Center** (p108) concert, then face a Dead Reckoning – a knockout rum cocktail at **Smuggler's Cove** (p105).

Day Four

☀ Wander 24th St past mural-covered bodegas and bookstores to **Balmy Alley** (p118), where this Mission muralist revival began. Stop for 'secret breakfast' (bourbon and cornflake) ice cream at **Humphry Slocombe** (p122), then continue to **Ritual Coffee Roasters** (p124). Pause for pirate supplies at **826 Valencia** (p118) and then duck into **Clarion Alley** (p114), the Mission's outdoor graffiti-art gallery. Passing Spanish adobe **Mission Dolores** (p118), salute the memorial hut to the native Ohlone and Miwok who built SF's first landmark.

☼ After carb-loading at **Pizzeria Delfina** (p121), nap in sunny **Dolores Park** (p115). Spot outrageous Victorian 'Painted Lady' houses on your way to hilltop **Alamo Square Park** (p136) for downtown vistas. Follow Panhandle park toward the Hippie Hill drum circle, then window-shop Haight St past record stores, vintage emporiums and **Bound Together Anarchist Book Collective** (p141).

☾ Place orders at **Rosamunde Sausage Grill** (p137) to enjoy with your pick of 400 microbrews at **Toronado** (p138). Don't miss showtime at deco-fabulous **Castro Theatre** (p131), where shows begin with a crowd sing-along.

Need to Know

For more information,
see Survival Guide (p183)

Currency
US dollar ($)

Language
English

Visas
The US Visa Waiver Program allows
nationals of 38 countries to enter the US
without a visa.

Money
ATMs widely available; credit cards
accepted at most hotels, stores and
restaurants. Many farmers market stalls,
food trucks and some bars are cash only.

Cell Phones
Most US cell phones besides the iPhone
operate on CDMA, not European-standard
GSM; check compatibility with your phone
service provider.

Time
Pacific Standard Time (GMT/UTC minus
eight hours)

Plugs & Adapters
Most plugs have two flat pins, some
appliances have two flat pins plus a round pin;
electrical current is 110-115V.

Tipping
At restaurants, 15% (bad service) to 25%
(exceptional service). Count on $1 to $2 per
drink at bars, $2 per bag to hotel porters, 15%
or $1 minimum per taxi ride.

① Before You Go

Your Daily Budget

Budget less than $150
▶ Dorm bed $30–$50
▶ Burrito $6–$9
▶ California Academy of Sciences
NightLife Thursdays $12

Midrange $150–$250
▶ Motel/home-share $125–$180
▶ Ferry Building meal $15–$40
▶ Alcatraz tour $30
▶ Oasis drag show $10–$30

Top End more than $250
▶ Boutique hotel $180–$380
▶ Chef's tasting menu $65–$228
▶ Opera orchestra seats $90–$135

Useful Websites

▶ **Lonely Planet** (www.lonelyplanet.com/
usa/san-francisco) Expert local advice.

▶ **7x7** (www.7x7.com) Trend-spotting SF
restaurants, bars and style.

▶ **SFGate** (www.sfgate.com) *San Francisco
Chronicle* news, events and restaurants.

Advance Planning

Two months before Book hotels and
Alcatraz tours for May to September; walk to
build stamina for hills.

Three weeks before Book Precita Eyes Mission mural and Chinatown Alleyways tours;
reserve for dinner at Rich Table, Benu or Coi.

One week before Look for tickets to American Conservatory Theater, San Francisco
Symphony or San Francisco Opera shows.

② Arriving in San Francisco

Service from three airports makes reaching San Francisco quick and convenient. BART offers easy access to downtown San Francisco from SFO and Oakland airports; from San Jose airport, shuttles connect to Caltrain. Amtrak trains are a low-emissions, scenic option for domestic travel to San Francisco.

✈ From San Francisco International Airport (SFO)

Destination	Best Transport
Downtown/Mission	BART
Rest of SF	Taxi/door-to-door shuttle

✈ From Oakland International Airport (OAK)

Destination	Best Transport
Downtown/Mission	BART
Rest of SF	Taxi/door-to-door shuttle

✈ At the Airports

San Francisco International Airport All terminals have ATMs, and there is a currency exchange in the international terminal. The airport's free AirTrain connects to the SFO BART station. Taxis depart outside baggage claim; shared vans depart from the marked curbside upstairs.

Oakland International Airport ATMs are available throughout the airport. Taxis, door-to-door shared vans leave curbside; BART connects Oakland airport to downtown and the Mission.

③ Getting Around

Small, hilly San Francisco is walkable, with public transportation and occasional taxis or bikes for backup. For transit options, departures and arrivals, check www.511.org or call ☎511. A detailed *Muni Street & Transit Map* is available free online (www.sfmta.com).

🚋 Cable Cars

Frequent, slow and scenic, from 6am to 1am daily; joyride from downtown to Chinatown, North Beach and Fisherman's Wharf. Single rides cost $7; for frequent use, get a Muni Passport (per day $17).

Ⓜ Muni Streetcar

Lines connect downtown and SoMa with Golden Gate Park, the Mission and the Castro. Historic F-line streetcars run from Fisherman's Wharf down Market St to the Castro. Fares are $2.25.

🚌 Muni Bus

Reasonably fast, but schedules vary wildly by line. Fares are $2.25.

Ⓑ BART Subway

High-speed transit from downtown to Civic Center, the Mission, Oakland/Berkeley, SFO and Millbrae, where it connects with Caltrain. Fares run $1.85 to $9.25.

🚗 Taxi

Fares run about $2.75 per mile; meters start at $3.50.

San Francisco Neighborhoods

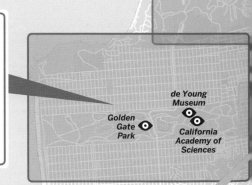

Golden Gate Bridge & the Marina (p22)
In full view of San Francisco's iconic landmark, you'll find Yoda, Disney, nature and nudity.

⊙ **Top Sights**
Golden Gate Bridge

Golden Gate Park & the Avenues (p142)
SF's Wild West is where the bison roam, penguins waddle, hippies drum and surfers rip.

⊙ **Top Sights**
Golden Gate Park

California Academy of Sciences

de Young Museum

Worth a Trip
⊙ **Top Sights**
Alcatraz (p48)

Exploratorium (p50)

Golden Gate Bridge

de Young Museum

Golden Gate Park

California Academy of Sciences

The Haight & NoPa (p132)
Sixties flashbacks, radical fashion, free music and pricey skateboards.

Fisherman's Wharf & the Piers (p34)
Adventures with sea lions and Space Invaders, submarine dives and Alcatraz escapes.

⊙ Top Sights
Fisherman's Wharf

Alcatraz ⊙

North Beach & Chinatown (p52)
Dragon gates and dim sum on one end of Grant St, parrots and espresso on the other – and poetry in every alley.

⊙ Top Sights
Coit Tower & Filbert Street Steps

⊙ *Fisherman's Wharf*

Coit Tower & Filbert Street Steps ⊙

⊙ *Exploratorium*

⊙ *Ferry Building*

⊙ *Cable Cars*

Asian Art Museum ⊙

Downtown & SoMa (p72)
Flagship stores and museum shows by day, underground clubs and Bay Bridge lights by night.

⊙ Top Sights
Ferry Building

Cable Cars

Hayes Valley & Civic Center (p96)
Grand buildings and great performances, foodie finds and local designs.

⊙ Top Sights
Asian Art Museum

The Mission (p112)
A book in one hand, a burrito in the other, murals all around.

Explore
San Francisco

View of Coit Tower (p54) and Alcatraz (p48)
LATITUDESTOCK-TTL / GETTY IMAGES ©

Explore

Golden Gate Bridge & the Marina

The waterfront neighborhood near Golden Gate Bridge has chic boutiques, outrageous theater, and food trucks in a former army depot – but 120 years ago it reeked of dirty laundry and drunken cows (swanky Union St was once Cow Hollow, where clothes were cleaned and cows munched mash from whiskey stills). Today's spiffy Mexdeco Marina was mostly built in the 1930s atop 1906 quake debris.

The Sights in a Day

☀ Browse boutiques for local designs and stylish bargains on Union and Chestnut Sts. Head to **Fort Mason** (pictured left; p31) for organic **Greens** (p29) chili takeout by the bayfront docks, then coffee at the **Interval** (p30) bar under Brian Eno's trippy digital paintings.

☀ Wander the Marina waterfront, from the **Wave Organ** (p28) past picturesque **Palace of Fine Arts** (p28) and into **Crissy Field** (p28) for sweeping Golden Gate Bridge views. Pop into the **Warming Hut** (p30) for nature-book browsing, or hike onward to Civil War–era **Fort Point** (p25) for a Hitchcock-worthy view of the bridge's ribbed orange underbelly. If you've got another couple of miles in you before sunset, walk across the **Golden Gate Bridge** (p24).

☾ Take the bus back toward Union St to hit happy hour at **West Coast Wine & Cheese** (p31) before your reservations at **A16** (p29). Enjoy a performance at **Magic Theatre** (p32), or take the stage yourself at **BATS Improv** (p32).

👁 Top Sight
Golden Gate Bridge (p24)

💜 Best of San Francisco

Outdoors
Crissy Field (p28)

Baker Beach (p28)

Architecture
Golden Gate Bridge (p24)

Palace of Fine Arts (p28)

Bargain Gourmet
Off the Grid (p31)

Entertainment
Fort Mason (p31)

Getting There

🚌 **Bus** Buses 47 and 49 connect the Marina to downtown; 41, 30 and 45 run to North Beach; 43 connects to the Haight; 22 runs to the Mission.

🚗 **Car** There's parking at Fort Mason and Crissy Field, and free parking in the adjoining Presidio.

Top Sights
Golden Gate Bridge

Strange but true: San Francisco's iconic orange suspension bridge was almost nixed by the Navy in favor of yellow-striped concrete pylons. Joseph B Strauss is the engineering mastermind behind the 1937 marvel, but architects Gertrude and Irving Murrow get credit for the soaring deco design and custom 'International Orange' color. Before the War Department could insist on an eyesore, laborers braved treacherous riptides and got to work, constructing the 1.7-mile span and 746ft suspension towers in just four years.

👁 Map p26, A1

www.goldengatebridge.org/visitors

off Lincoln Blvd

northbound free, southbound toll $6; for details, see www.goldengate.org/tolls

🚌 28, all Golden Gate Transit buses

Golden Gate Bridge

Don't Miss

Vista Points

San Franciscans have passionate perspectives on every subject, but especially their signature landmark. Fog aficionados prefer the north-end lookout at Marin's Vista Point to watch clouds tumble over bridge cables. Crissy Field is a key spot to appreciate the span in its entirety, with windsurfers and kite-fliers adding action to your snapshots. From clothing-optional Baker Beach, you can see the bridge's backside in all its naked glory.

Fort Point

Completed in 1861 with 126 cannons, **Fort Point** (☏415-556-1693; www.nps.gov/fopo; Marine Dr; admission free; ⊙10am-5pm Fri-Sun; ℗; ➓28) stood guard against certain invasion by Confederate soldiers during the Civil War...or not. This heavily armed fort saw no action – at least until Alfred Hitchcock shot scenes from *Vertigo* here, with stunning views of the Golden Gate Bridge from below. Enter the fortress to check out 19th-century historical displays – including surprisingly tasty military menus – and climb to rooftop viewing decks for close-up glimpses of the bridge's underbelly, and hear the whoosh of traffic overhead.

Bridge Crossings

To see both sides of the Golden Gate, hike or bike the span. From the parking area and bus stop, a pedestrian pathway leads past the toll plaza to the east sidewalk (pedestrian access 5am to 6:30pm daily). Near the toll plaza is a cross-section of suspension cable, with the tensile strength to support thousands of cars and buses daily. If you'd rather not walk back, Golden Gate Transit buses head back to SF from Marin. Bikes have 24-hour bridge access via either sidewalk, but must yield to pedestrians on the east sidewalk. Electric bikes must be powered down during bridge crossings.

☑ Top Tips

▸ Carpools (three or more) are free 5am to 9am and 4pm to 6pm.

▸ Dress warmly before crossing the bridge on foot or bike, with a water-resistant outer layer to break the wind and fog.

▸ Skating and pets (except guide animals) are not allowed on bridge sidewalks. Wheelchairs are permitted on the east sidewalk.

▸ Glimpse the underbelly of the bridge from the Municipal Pier in front of the Warming Hut. By reservation Saturday mornings March to October, Fort Point staff demonstrate how to catch crabs here.

✗ Take a Break

Stop by the certified-green Warming Hut (p30) for fair-trade coffee and pastries.

A B C D

1

San Francisco
Bay

Golden Gate
Bridge

**Golden Gate
Bridge** ◉

Marine Dr. ⊗ 12

US Hwy 101

Long Ave

Crissy
Field ◉ 1

2

101

Armistead Rd

Presidio Pkwy

Old Mason St 🔒
20

Storey Ave

Lincoln Blvd

Ralston Ave

Upton Ave

San Francisco
National
Military
Cemetery

Montgomery St

Anza Ave

Lincoln Blvd

Keyes Ave

3

▣ 2
**Baker
Beach**

Kobbe Ave

**MAIN
POST**

Moraga Ave

Funston Ave

Hunter Rd

**Presidio
National
Park**

Washington Rd

PRESIDIO

Park Blvd

1

4 ◉ **Presidio of
San Francisco**

Washington Blvd

Pershing
Square

⊗ 10

Hardie Ave

Macarthur Ave

Quarry Rd

4

Compton Rd

Water
Reservoir

Arguello Blvd

Arguello Blvd

5

1

**Presidio
Golf
Course**

Maple St

Pacific Ave

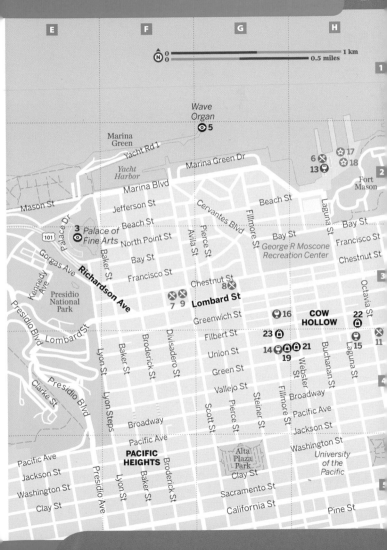

Sights

Crissy Field   PARK

1 ◎ Map p26, D2

War is for the birds at Crissy Field, a military airstrip turned waterfront nature preserve with knockout Golden Gate views. Where military aircraft once zoomed in for landings, bird-watchers now huddle in the silent rushes of a reclaimed tidal marsh. Joggers pound beachside trails and the only security alerts are raised by puppies suspiciously sniffing surfers. On foggy days, stop by the certified-green Warming Hut (p30) to browse regional-nature books and warm up with fair-trade coffee. (www.crissyfield.org; 1199 East Beach; **P**; ☐30, PresidioGo Shuttle)

Baker Beach   BEACH

2 ◎ Map p26, A3

Picnic amid wind-sculpted pines, fish from craggy rocks or frolic nude at mile-long Baker Beach, with spectacular views of the bridge. Crowds come weekends, especially on fog-free days; arrive early. For nude sunbathing (mostly straight girls and gay boys), head to the northern end. Families in clothing stick to the southern end, nearer the parking lot. Mind the currents and the c-c-cold water. (☼sunrise-sunset; **P**; ☐29, PresidioGo Shuttle)

Palace of Fine Arts   MONUMENT

3 ◎ Map p26, E3

Like a fossilized party favor, this romantic, ersatz Greco-Roman ruin

is the city's memento from the 1915 Panama-Pacific International Exposition. The original was built of wood, burlap and plaster, designed by celebrated Berkeley architect Bernard Maybeck, then later reinforced. By the 1960s it was crumbling. The structure was recast in concrete, so future generations could gaze up at the rotunda relief to glimpse 'Art under attack by materialists, with idealists leaping to her rescue.' (www.lovethepalace.org; Palace Dr; admission free; ☐28, 30, 43)

Presidio of San Francisco   PARK

4 ◎ Map p26, C4

Explore that splotch of green on the map between Baker Beach and Crissy Field, and you'll find a parade grounds, Yoda, a centuries-old adobe wall and some thrilling site-specific art installations. What started out as a Spanish fort built by conscripted Ohlone in 1776 is now a treasure hunt of surprises. (☎415-561-4323; www.nps.gov/prsf; ☼dawn-dusk; **P**; ☐28, 43)

Wave Organ   MONUMENT

5 ◎ Map p26, G2

A project of the Exploratorium (p50), the Wave Organ is a sound sculpture of PVC tubes and concrete pipes capped with found marble from San Francisco's old cemetery, built into the tip of the yacht-harbor jetty. Depending on the waves, winds and tide, the tones emitted sound like nervous humming from a dinnertime line-chef or spooky heavy breathing over the phone in a slasher

film. (www.exploratorium.edu/visit/wave
-organ; Marina Small Craft Harbor jetty; admission
free; ☼daylight hours; ♿; 🚌22, 30)

Eating

Greens
VEGETARIAN, CALIFORNIAN **$$**

6 🍴 Map p26, H2

Career carnivores won't realize there's
zero meat in the hearty black-bean
chili, or in the other flavor-packed
vegetarian dishes, made using ingredients
from a Zen farm in Marin. And
oh, what views – the Golden Gate rises
just outside the window-lined dining
room. The on-site café serves to-go
lunches. For sit-down meals, including
Sunday brunch, reservations are essential.
(📞415-771-6222; www.greens
restaurant.com; Bldg A, Fort Mason Center, cnr
Marina Blvd & Laguna St; lunch $15-18, dinner
$18-25; ☼11:45am-2:30pm & 5:30-9pm Tue-Fri,
from 11am Sat, 10:30am-2pm & 5:30-9pm
Sun, 5:30-9pm Mon; 🍴♿; 🚌28)

A16
ITALIAN **$$$**

7 🍴 Map p26, F3

Even before A16 won a James Beard
Award, it was hard to book, but
persevere: the housemade mozzarella
burrata, blister-crusted pizzas from
the wood-burning oven, and 12-page
Italian wine list make it worth your
while. Skip the spotty desserts and
instead double up on adventurous
appetizers, including house-cured
salumi platters and delectable
marinated tuna. (📞415-771-2216; www.

Food truck at Off the Grid (p31)

a16sf.com; 2355 Chestnut St; pizza $13-19,
mains $21-36; ☼11:30am-2:30pm Wed-Fri,
5:30-10pm Mon-Thu, to 11pm Fri, 5-11pm Sat,
to 10pm Sun; 🚌28, 30, 43)

Blue Barn Gourmet
SANDWICHES, SALADS **$**

8 🍴 Map p26, G3

Toss aside ordinary salads. For $11.75,
build a mighty mound of organic produce,
topped with six fixings: artisan
cheeses, caramelized onions, heirloom
tomatoes, candied pecans, pomegranate
seeds, even Meyer grilled sirloin.
For something hot, try toasted panini
oozing with Manchego cheese, fig jam
and salami. (📞415-441-3232; www.blue
barngourmet.com; 2105 Chestnut St; salads &

sandwiches $10-14; ⊙11am-8:30pm Mon-Thu, to 8pm Fri-Sun; 🚴🏻; 🚍22, 28, 30, 43)

Mamacita MEXICAN $$

9 Map p26, F3

One of the city's best for sit-down Mexican, Mamacita makes everything from scratch – tortillas, tamales and two dozen fresh-daily sauces for wide-ranging dishes, from spit-roasted goat to duck *carnitas*. The knock-out cocktail menu lists 60 tequilas, which explains the room's deafening roar. Make reservations. (📞415-346-8494; www.mamacitasf.com; 2317 Chestnut St; items $10-18; ⊙5:30pm-late Mon-Thu, 5pm-late Fri-Sun; 🚍30)

Arguello MEXICAN $$

10 Map p26, D4

Inside the Presidio Officers' Club, this Mexican restaurant, by James Beard Award–winner Traci Des Jardins, features small dishes good for sharing, plus several mains, including standout caramelized pork shoulder. The bar makes great margaritas, which you can sip fireside in the adjoining Moraga Hall, former officers' club lounge. (📞415-561-3650; www.arguellosf. com; 50 Moraga Ave; mains $12-18; ⊙11am-9pm Wed-Sat, brunch to 4pm Sun; 📶; 🚍43, PresidiGo Shuttle)

Roam Artisan Burger BURGERS $

11 Map p26, H4

Obsessive about ingredients, Roam serves burgers of beef, bison and turkey, all locally grown and sustainably farmed. For classics, stick to juicy grass-fed beef served on a fresh-baked bun with housemade pickles. Don't ask for Coke: Roam makes its own organic sodas, plus stellar milkshakes with ice cream from Sonoma. (📞415-440-7626; www.roamburgers.com; 1785 Union St; burgers $8-10; ⊙11:30am-10pm; 🚴🏻; 🚍41, 45)

Warming Hut CAFÉ, SANDWICHES $

12 Map p26, B2

Wetsuited windsurfers and Crissy Field kite-fliers recharge with fair-trade coffee, organic pastries and hot dogs at the Warming Hut, while browsing field guides and sampling honey from Presidio honeybees. Ingeniously insulated with recycled denim, this eco-shack below the Golden Gate Bridge evolved from a heartwarming concept: all purchases fund Crissy Field's ongoing conversion from US army airstrip to wildlife preserve. (📞415-561-3040; 983 Marine Dr, Presidio; items $4-6; ⊙9am-5pm; 🅿🚴🏻; 🚍PresidiGo Shuttle)

Drinking

Interval Bar & Cafe BAR

13 Map p26, H2

Designed to stimulate discussion of philosophy and art, the Interval is our favorite spot in the Marina for cocktails and conversation. It's inside the Long Now Foundation, with floor-to-ceiling bookshelves, which contain the canon of Western lit, rising above a glorious 10,000-year clock – fitting backdrop for aged Tom Collins, daiquiris and gimlets, or single-origin coffee, tea and snacks. (www.theinterval.org; Fort Mason Center, Bldg A, 2 Marina Blvd; ⏲10am-midnight; 🚌28, 30)

West Coast Wine & Cheese
WINE BAR

14 Map p26, G4

A rack of 720 bottles frames the wall at this austerely elegant storefront wine bar, which exclusively wines from California, Oregon and Washington, 26 by the glass. All pair with delectable small bites, including octopus a la plancha, charcuterie and cheese plates. Weekends (11am to 2:30pm) there's excellent brunch – with bubbles, naturally. (www.westcoastsf.com; 2165 Union St; dishes $9-21; ⏲4-10pm Mon-Fri, 11am-10pm Sat & Sun; 🚌22, 41, 45)

Lightning Tavern
BAR

15 🍸 Map p26, H4

Edison-bulb chandeliers and laboratory equipment lend a mad-scientist backdrop for bartenders, who serve good beers and cocktails, also available by the pitcher (think messy night out). Good pub grub – including 'totchos,' tater-tot nachos – keep your buzz in check. (📞415-704-1875; 1875 Union St; ⏲4pm-2am Mon-Fri, 10am-2am Sat & Sun; 🚌41, 45)

MatrixFillmore
LOUNGE

16 🍸 Map p26, G3

The neighborhood's most notorious upmarket pick-up joint provides a fascinating glimpse into the lives of single Marina swankers. Treat it as a comic sociological study, while enjoying stellar cocktails, a blazing fireplace and sexy lounge beats – if, that is, you can get past the door. Bring your credit card. (www.matrixfillmore.com; 3138 Fillmore St; ⏲8pm-2am Wed-Mon; 🚌22, 28, 30, 43)

 Local Life
Off the Grid at Fort Mason
On Friday evenings at **Fort Mason** (Map p26, H2; 📞415-345-7500; www.fortmason.org; cnr Marina Blvd & Laguna St; 🅿; 🚌22, 28, 30) – a former shipyard that was the embarkation point for WWII Pacific troops – up to 30 trucks gather for **Off the Grid** (Map p26, H2; www.offthegridsf.com; items $5-12; ⏲Fort Mason Center 5-10pm Fri Apr-Oct, Presidio 5-9pm Thu & 11am-4pm Sun Apr-Oct; 👶; 🚌22, 28), SF's biggest mobile-gourmet hootenanny. Arrive before 6:30pm for best selections and shorter lines for roast duck buns from the **Chairman**, free-range roast chicken from **Roli Roti**, and dessert from the **Créme Brûlée Man**. Thursday evenings and Sundays at midday, spring through fall, you can also hit Off the Grid at the Presidio's Main Post Lawn, and join the epic picnic on the former Army parade grounds.

Entertainment

Magic Theatre
THEATER

17 Map p26, H2

The Magic is known for taking risks and staging provocative plays by playwrights such as Bill Pullman, Terrence McNally, Edna O'Brien, David Mamet and longtime playwright-in-residence Sam Shepard. If you're interested in seeing new theatrical works and getting under the skin of the Bay Area theater scene, the Magic is an excellent starting point. Check the calendar. (☎415-441-8822; www.magictheatre.org; 3rd fl, Bldg D, Fort Mason Center, cnr Marina Blvd & Laguna St; tickets $30-60; ☒28)

BATS Improv
THEATER

18 Map p26, H2

Bay Area Theater Sports explores all things improv, from audience-inspired themes to whacked-out musicals at completely improvised weekend shows. Or take center stage yourself at an improv-comedy workshop (held on weekday nights and weekend afternoons). Think fast: classes fill quickly. Admission prices vary depending on the show/workshop. (☎415-474-8935; www.improv.org; 3rd fl, Bldg B, Fort Mason Center, cnr Marina Blvd & Laguna St; tickets $17-20; ☻shows 8pm Fri & Sat; ☒28)

Shopping

ATYS
HOUSEWARES, GIFTS

19 Map p26, G4

Tucked in a courtyard, this design showcase is like a museum store for exceptional, artistic household items – to wit, a mirrored coat rack, a rechargeable flashlight that turns a wineglass into a lamp, and a zero-emissions, solar-powered toy airplane. Expect sleek, modern designs of superior quality that you won't find anywhere else. (www.atysdesign.com; 2149B Union St; ☻11am-6:30pm Mon-Sat, noon-6pm Sun; ☒22, 41, 45)

Sports Basement
OUTDOOR GEAR

20 Map p26, C3

Specializing in odd lots of sporting goods at closeout prices, this 80,000 sq-ft sports-and-camping emporium is also the best place to rent wetsuits for swims at Aquatic Park, gear for last-minute trips to Yosemite, or bikes to cross the nearby GG bridge – and free parking makes it easy to trade your rental car for a bike. (☎415-437-0100; www.sportsbasement.com; 610 Old Mason St; ☻9am-9pm Mon-Fri, 8am-8pm Sat & Sun; ☒30, 43, PresidiGo Shuttle (Crissy Field Route))

Sui Generis Illa
CLOTHING

21 Map p26, H4

Sui generis is latin for one of a kind – which is what you'll find at this high-end designer consignment shop that features recent seasons' looks, one-of-

LISSANDRA MELO / SHUTTERSTOCK ©

Palace of Fine Arts (p28)

a-kind gowns and a few archival pieces by key couturiers from decades past. No jeans, no pants – unless they're leather or super-glam. Yes, it's pricy, but far cheaper than you'd pay shopping retail. (☏415-800-4584; www.suigeneris consignment.com; 2147 Union St; ⏱11am-7pm Mon-Sat, to 5pm Sun; 🚌22, 41, 45)

Ambiance
ACCESSORIES, FASHION

22 🔒 Map p26, H3

The Union St outpost of this three-store, SF-based chain showcases midrange designers, with a good mix of trendy and classic cuts in jeans, dresses, shirts, shoes and locally made jewelry. Half the store is devoted to sale items, at least 20% below retail,

sometimes yielding great bargains. (www.ambiancesf.com; 1858 Union St; ⏱11am-8pm Mon-Fri, 10am-8pm Sat, 11am-7pm Sun; 🚌41, 45)

My Roommate's Closet
WOMEN'S CLOTHING

23 🔒 Map p26, G4

All the half-off bargains and none of the clawing dangers of a sample sale. Stocks constantly change but have included cloud-like Catherine Malandrino chiffon party dresses, executive Diane Von Fürstenberg wrap dresses, and designer denim at prices approaching reality. (www.shopmrc.com; 3044 Fillmore St; ⏱11am-7pm Mon-Sat, noon-5:30pm Sun; 🚌22, 41, 45)

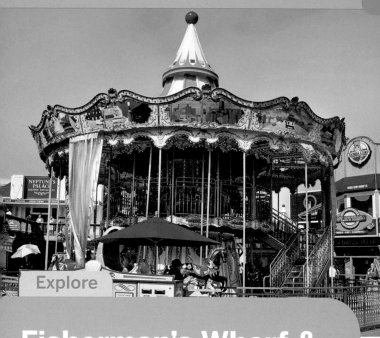

Explore

Fisherman's Wharf & the Piers

The waterfront that today welcomes families fresh off the boat from Alcatraz tours was a dodgy dock area during California's Gold Rush. After the 1906 earthquake and fire, a retaining wall was built, and Sunday strollers gradually replaced drifters and grifters along Embarcadero boardwalks. But Wild West manners prevail on Pier 39, where sea lions snore and belch like drunken sailors dockside.

The Sights in a Day

☀️ Escapees from Alcatraz flee the piers fast – but families might be held captive by Pier 39's kid-friendly attractions, especially **Aquarium of the Bay** (p38) and **San Francisco Carousel** (pictured left; p39). Otherwise, salute Pier 39's resident **sea lions** (p37) dockside, and race boardwalk crowds to an early lunch at **Codmother Fish & Chips** (p44).

☀️ Recover from the inevitable starch stupor by saving the world from Space Invaders and playing steampunk arcade games at **Musée Mécanique** (p37), then enter stealth mode on an actual WWII submarine: the **USS Pampanito** (p37). Back on dry land, explore 1930s murals inside the shipshape **Maritime Museum** (p41) and warm up with Irish coffee at **Buena Vista Cafe** (p46). Hop off the Hyde St cable car at wiggly **Lombard St** (p41) for poetry-inspiring Golden Gate vistas, and glimpse a master muralist at work in the San Francisco fresco-within-a-fresco at **Diego Rivera Gallery** (p42).

🌙 For dinner, go high or low: **Gary Danko** (p43) for award-winning California cuisine or fast food at **In-N-Out Burger** (p44).

👁️ Top Sights

Marine Life at Fisherman's Wharf (p36)

❤️ Best of San Francisco

Freebies

Maritime Museum (p41)

Sea Lions at Pier 39 (p37)

Kids

Musée Mécanique (p37)

Sea Lions at Pier 39 (p37)

Aquarium of the Bay (p38)

Fine Dining

Gary Danko (p43)

Museums & Galleries

USS Pampanito (p37)

Maritime Museum (p41)

Getting There

Ⓜ️ **Streetcar** Historic F Market streetcars connect the Wharf with the Castro via downtown.

🚡 **Cable car** Powell-Hyde and Powell-Mason lines head from downtown to the Wharf.

🚌 **Bus** Wharf–downtown buses include 30, 47 and 49.

🚗 **Car** Park at public garages at Pier 39 and Ghirardelli Square.

Top Sights
Marine Life at Fisherman's Wharf

Where fishermen once snared sea creatures, San Francisco now traps tourists in a commercial sprawl between the cable car terminus and the Alcatraz Cruises port. But where you'd least expect it, Fisherman's Wharf offers surprise and delight. Here you can sunbathe with sea lions, ride carousel unicorns, experience stealth mode inside a WWII submarine, consult 100-year-old fortune-tellers, and watch sharks circle from the safety of glass tubes built right into the bay.

◉ Map p18

www.fishermanswharf.org

Embarcadero & Jefferson St waterfront, from Pier 29 to Van Ness Ave

🚌 19, 30, 47, 49, 🚋 Powell-Mason, Powell-Hyde, Ⓜ F

Sea lions at Pier 39

Don't Miss

Sea Lions at Pier 39

Rock stars wish they could live like San Francisco's sea lions, who've taken over an entire yacht marina with their harems since 1990. Since California law requires boats to make way for marine mammals, up to 1300 sea-lion squatters oblige yacht-owners to relinquish **Pier 39** (☎981-1280; www.pier39.com; Beach St & the Embarcadero; ☺Jan-Jul & whenever else they feel like it; ᯉ15, 37, 49, ⓂF) slips from January through July. With loud guffaws on yacht docks, these beach bums seem positively gleeful about it.

Musée Mécanique

Laughing Sal has freaked out visitors with her coin-operated cackle for 100 years, but don't let this manic mannequin deter you from the best arcade in the west. With a few quarters at the **Musée Mécanique** (☎415-346-2000; www.musee-mechanique.org; Pier 45, Shed A; ☺10am-7pm Mon-Fri, to 8pm Sat & Sun; ♿; ᯉ47, ᯈPowell-Mason, Powell-Hyde, ⓂF), you can start bar brawls in mechanical Wild West saloons, save the world from Space Invaders and get your fortune told by an eerily lifelike wooden swami.

USS Pampanito

Dive, dive, dive! Head into the belly of a restored **WWII US Navy submarine** (☎415-775-1943, tickets 855-384-6410; www.maritime.org/pamphome.htm; Pier 45; adult/child $12/6, plus audio tour $3; ☺9am-8pm Thu-Tue, to 6pm Wed; ♿; ᯉ19, 30, 47, ᯈPowell-Hyde, ⓂF) that sunk six Japanese ships (including two carrying British and Australian POWs). Submariners' stories of tense moments in underwater stealth mode will have you holding your breath – caution, claustrophobes – and all those brass

☑ Top Tips

► Afternoon fog blows in around 4pm, sometimes earlier in summer. Carry a jacket and don't wear shorts, except in a rare heat wave.

► Most people cover waterfront attractions on foot or bike – wear comfortable shoes and sunscreen.

► Fisherman's Wharf is most popular with families, who pack the waterfront by early afternoon. To dodge the crowds, arrive at Pier 43½ seafood shacks early for lunch and visit the USS *Pampanito* and Maritime Museum in the afternoon.

✗ Take a Break

Snack shacks line the Pier 39 boardwalk and flank picnic benches at Pier 43½, including Fisherman's Wharf Crab Stands (p44). To treat/bribe kids, try Kara's Cupcakes (p43).

knobs and hydraulic valves make 21st-century technology seem overrated.

Aquarium of the Bay

Take a long walk off a short pier right into the bay, and stay perfectly safe and dry as sharks circle, manta rays flutter and schools of fish flit over-head. The **aquarium** (www.aquarium ofthebay.org; Pier 39; adult/child/family $21.95/12.95/64; ☺9am-8pm late May-early Sep, shorter off-season hours; ★; ☐49, ☐Powell-Mason, ⓂF) is built into the bay, with a conveyor belt transport-ing you through underwater glass tubes for an up-close look at local aquaculture.

San Francisco Maritime National Historic Park

'Aye, she's a beauty,' you'll growl like a salty dog aboard **historic ships** (www. nps.gov/safr; 499 Jefferson St, Hyde St Pier; 7-day ticket adult/child $5/free; ☺9:30am-5pm Oct-May, to 5:30pm Jun-Sep; ★; ☐19, 30, 47, ☐Powell-Hyde, ⓂF) open as muse-ums along Hyde St Pier – especially el-egant 1891 schooner *Alma* and iconic c 1890 steamboat *Eureka*. Other boats resemble giant bath toys, including steam-powered paddlewheel tugboat *Eppleton Hall* and triple-masted, iron-hulled 1886 British *Balclutha,* which hauled coal to San Francisco via Cape Horn.

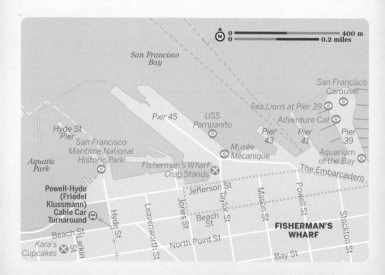

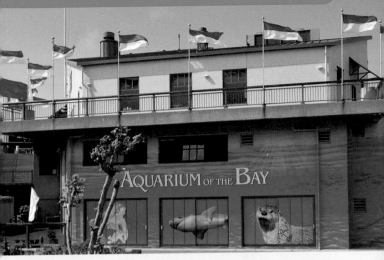

Aquarium of the Bay

San Francisco Carousel

Your chariot awaits to whisk you and the kids past the Golden Gate Bridge, Alcatraz and other SF landmarks hand-painted onto this Italian **carousel** (www.pier39.com; Pier 39; admission $3; ⏱11am-7pm; 📷; 🚌47, 🚋Powell-Mason, ⓂF), twinkling with 1800 lights. Old-timey organ carnival music inspires goofy sing-alongs on the four-minute ride.

Adventure Cat

Centuries of sailors are right: there's no better view of San Francisco than from its silvery bay, especially on a sunset sail. **Adventure Cat** (📞415-777-1630; www.adventurecat.com; Pier 39; adult/child $40/20, sunset cruise $55; 📷; 🚌47, ⓂF) lets you sail off into the sunset on catamaran cruises with dazzling bay views, trampolines between hulls for bouncy kids and windless cabins in case of fog (dress warmly). Three daily cruises depart March to October; weekends only in November.

San Francisco Bay

Ferries to Alcatraz

Pier 31

18

Sansome St

Pier 33

Pier 35

Kearny St

Pioneer Park/ Greenwich St

Telegraph Hill

Filbert St Steps

Alta St

For reviews see

Top Sights	p36
Sights	p41
Eating	p43
Drinking	p46
Entertainment	p46
Shopping	p47

The Embarcadero (Herb Caen Way)

North Point St

Beach St

Bay St

Francisco St

Chestnut St

Lombard St

Stockton St

Grant Ave

Jasper Pl

Columbus Ave

NORTH BEACH

Green St

Vallejo St

Pier 39

Powell St

Washington Square

North Beach Playground

9

Pier 41

Ferries to Sausalito

Jefferson St

FISHERMAN'S WHARF

Mason St

Powell-Mason Cable Car Turnaround

Pier 43

Red & White Fleet

6

17

Taylor St

Water St

14

Greenwich St

Filbert St

Union St

Macondray Ln

Ina Coolbrith Park

NOB HILL

Green St

SS Jeremiah O'Brien

Pier 45

13

Marine Life at Fisherman's Wharf

15 11

Jones St

Columbus Ave

Diego Rivera Gallery

3

1 Lombard Street

RUSSIAN HILL

4

10

Pier 47

12

Beach St

Golden Gate National Recreation Area Headquarters

Leavenworth St

Jefferson St

Hyde St

Aquatic Park

5

Powell-Hyde (Friedel Klussmann) Cable Car Turnaround

16 7

George Sterling Park

Bay St Russian Hill Park

Larkin St

San Francisco Municipal Pier

Maritime Museum

2

Ghirardelli Square

20 19 8

North Point St

Polk St

Van Ness Ave

Francisco St

Chestnut St

Lombard St

Greenwich St

Filbert St

Van Ness Ave

400 m

0.2 miles

MARK BOSTER / GETTY IMAGES ©

Lombard Street

Sights

Lombard Street
STREET

1 ⊙ Map p40, B3

You've seen its eight switchbacks in a thousand photographs. The tourist board has dubbed this 'the world's crookedest street,' which is factually incorrect. Vermont St in Potrero Hill deserves that award, but Lombard is much more scenic, with its red-brick pavement and lovingly tended flower-beds. It wasn't always so bent; before the arrival of the automobile it lunged straight down the hill. (900 block of Lombard St; 🚃Powell-Hyde)

Maritime Museum
MUSEUM

2 ⊙ Map p40, A2

A monumental hint to sailors in need of a scrub, this restored, ship-shape 1939 streamline moderne landmark is decked out with Works Progress Administration (WPA) art treasures: playful seal and frog sculptures by Beniamino Bufano, Hilaire Hiler's surreal underwater dreamscape murals and recently uncovered wood reliefs by Richard Ayer. Acclaimed African American artist Sargent Johnson created the stunning carved green slate marquee doorway and the verandah's mesmerizing aquatic mosaics.

Johnson deliberately left unfinished the mosaics on the eastern side to protest plans to include a private restaurant in this public facility. Johnson won: the east wing is now a maritime museum office. (Aquatic Park Bathhouse; www.maritime.org; 900 Beach St; admission free; ⊗10am-4pm; ♦; 🚋19, 30, 47, 🚡Powell-Hyde)

Diego Rivera Gallery GALLERY

3 ◎ Map p40, B3

Diego Rivera's 1931 *The Making of a Fresco Showing a Building of a City* is a *trompe l'oeil* fresco within a fresco, showing the artist himself, pausing to admire his work, as well as the work in progress that is San Francisco. The fresco covers an entire wall in the Diego Rivera Gallery at the San Francisco Art Institute. For a memorable San Francisco aspect, head to the terrace café for espresso and panoramic bay views. (☎415-771-7020; www.sfai.edu; 800 Chestnut St; admission free; ⊗9am-7pm; 🚋30, 🚡Powell-Mason)

SS Jeremiah O'Brien HISTORIC SITE

4 ◎ Map p40, B1

Hard to believe this 10,000-ton beauty was turned out by San Francisco's ship workers in under eight weeks, and harder still to imagine how she dodged U-boats on a mission delivering supplies to Allied forces on D-Day. Of 2710 Liberty Ships launched during WWII, this is the only one still fully operational. For steamy piston-on-piston, 2700HP action, visit during 'steaming weekends' (usually the third weekend of the month, summertime) or check the website for upcoming four-hour cruises. (☎415-554-0100; www.ssjeremiahobrien.org; Pier 45; adult/child $12/6; ⊗9am-4pm; ♦; 🚋19, 30, 47, 🚡Powell-Hyde, Ⓜ F)

Aquatic Park PARK

5 ◎ Map p40, A2

Eccentricity along Fisherman's Wharf is mostly staged, but here it's the real deal: extreme swimmers dive from the concrete beachfront into the bloodcurdling waters of the bay in winter, weirdos mumble conspiracy theories on the grassy knoll of panoramic Victoria Park, and wistful tycoons stare off into the distance and contemplate sailing far away from their Blackberries. (northern end of Van Ness Ave; admission free; ♦; 🚋19, 30, 47, 🚡Powell-Hyde)

Red & White Fleet BAY CRUISE

6 ◎ Map p40, C1

A one-hour bay cruise with Red & White lets you see the Golden Gate Bridge from water level. Brave the wind and sit on the outdoor upper deck. Audio tours in multiple languages provide narrative. On-board alcohol subdues naysayers. (☎415-673-2900; www.redandwhite.com; Pier 43½; adult/child $30/20; ♦; 🚋47, Ⓜ F)

Eating

Gary Danko CALIFORNIAN $$$

7 ✖ Map p40, B2

Gary Danko wins James Beard Awards for his impeccable haute California cuisine. Smoked-glass windows prevent passersby from tripping over their tongues at the exquisite presentations – roasted lobster with trumpet mushrooms, blushing duck breast and rhubarb compote, lavish cheeses and trios of crèmes brûlées. Reservations a must. (📞415-749-2060; www.garydanko.com; 800 North Point St; 3-/5-course menu $81/117; ⏰5:30-10pm; 🚌19, 30, 47, 🚋Powell-Hyde)

Kara's Cupcakes BAKERY, DESSERT $

8 ✖ Map p40, A2

Proustian nostalgia washes over fully grown adults as they bite into cupcakes that recall childhood magician-led birthday parties. Varieties range from yummy chocolate marshmallow to classic carrot cake with cream-cheese frosting, all meticulously calculated for maximum glee – there's even gluten-free. (📞415-563-2253; www.karascupcakes.com; 900 North Point St; cupcakes $2–3.75; ⏰10am-8pm Sun-Thu, to 10pm Fri & Sat; 🚌28, 30, 49, 🚋Powell-Hyde, Powell-Mason)

Forbes Island GRILL $$$

9 ✖ Map p40, D1

No man is an island, except for an eccentric millionaire named Forbes Thor Kiddoo. A miniature lighthouse, thatched hut, waterfall, sandy beach and swaying palms transformed his moored houseboat into the Hearst Castle of the bay. Today this bizarre domicile is a gently rocking romantic restaurant, strong on grilled meats and atmosphere – consider the lamb lollipops. Reservations essential. (📞415-951-4900; www.forbesisland.com; Pier 41; 4-course menu $75; ⏰5pm-late; 🚻; 🚌47, Ⓜ F)

Scoma's

SEAFOOD **$$$**

10 Map p40, B1

Flashback to the 1960s, with waiters in white dinner jackets, pine-paneled walls decorated with signed photographs of forgotten celebrities, and plate-glass windows overlooking the docks – Scoma's is the Wharf's long-standing staple for seafood. Little changes except prices. Expect classics like cioppino and lobster Thermidor – never groundbreaking, always good – that taste better when someone else buys. (415-771-4383; www.scomas.com; Pier 47; mains $28-42; 11:30am-10pm; P; Powell-Hyde, MF)

Codmother Fish and Chips

FISH & CHIPS **$**

11 Map p40, B2

If being at Fisherman's Wharf makes you crave fish and chips, skip the expensive restaurants lining the water and instead find this little food truck, which makes delicious fried cod, Baja-style fish tacos, and several varieties of flavored French fries. Note the early closing time at dinner. (415-606-9349; 2824 Jones St; mains $5-10; 11:30am-7pm; 47, Powell-Mason, MF)

In-N-Out Burger

BURGERS **$**

12 Map p40, B2

Gourmet burgers have taken SF by storm, but In-N-Out has had a good thing going for 60 years: prime chuck beef processed on-site, plus fries and shakes made with ingredients you can pronounce, all served by employees paid a living wage. Consider ordering yours off the menu 'animal style,' cooked in mustard with grilled onions. (800-786-1000; www.in-n-out.com; 333 Jefferson St; meals under $10; 10:30am-1am Sun-Thu, to 1:30am Fri & Sat; ; 30, 47, Powell-Hyde)

Fisherman's Wharf Crab Stands

SEAFOOD **$**

13 Map p40, C1

Brawny-armed men stir steaming cauldrons of Dungeness crab at several side-by-side take-away crab stands at the foot of Taylor St, the epicenter of Fisherman's Wharf. Crab season typically runs winter through spring, but you'll find shrimp and other seafood year-round. (Foot of Taylor St; mains $5-15; MF)

✓ Top Tip

Sourdough Bread

San Francisco's climate isn't great for bikinis, but it's perfect for lactobacillus sanfranciscensis, the lactic-acid bacteria that gives sourdough bread its distinctive tang and helps activate yeast. Any self-respecting San Francisco bakery serves sourdough, but the most famous is **Boudin Bakery** (Map p40, C1; www.boudinbakery.com; 160 Jefferson St; items $7-15; 11am-9:30pm; 47, MF), a San Francisco institution since 1849.

DAVID PAUL MORRIS / GETTY IMAGES ©

Crab stand at Fisherman's Wharf

Pat's Cafe

AMERICAN $

14 Map p40, C3

Just beyond the tourist hubbub, this cute little storefront diner serves classic-American food – scrambles, pancakes and waffles for breakfast; hot pastrami, patty melts and club sandwiches for lunch – to locals and out-of-towners who appreciate no-fuss cooking, cheerful service and the easy location between the Wharf and North Beach. (☎415-776-8735; patscafesf.com; 2330 Taylor St; mains $8-12; ☺7:30am-2:30pm; 👶; 🚌30, 🚋Powell-Mason)

Carmel Pizza Co.

PIZZA $$

15 Map p40, B2

Remarkable that a food truck could contain a wood-burning oven, but herein lies the secret to Carmel Pizza's remarkably good single-serving blistered-crust pizzas. Note the early closing time at dinner. (☎415-676-1185; www.carmelpizzaco.com; 2826 Jones St; pizzas $11-18; ☺11:30am-3:30pm & 5-8pm Mon, Tue & Thu, noon-8pm Fri & Sat, to 6pm Sun; 🚌47, 🚋Powell-Mason, Ⓜ F)

Drinking

Buena Vista Cafe   BAR

16 🍷 Map p40, B2

Warm your cockles with a prim little goblet of bitter-creamy Irish coffee, introduced to America at this destination bar that once served sailors and cannery workers. The creaky Victorian floor manages to hold up carousers and families alike, served community-style at round tables overlooking the cable car turnaround at Victoria Park. (☎415-474-5044; www.thebuenavista.com; 2765 Hyde St; ⊙9am-2am Mon-Fri, 8am-2am Sat & Sun; 🛜; 🚌19, 47, 🚋Powell-Hyde)

 Top Tip

Blazing Saddles

To gear up for a Gary Danko feast, cover the waterfront from Pier 39 to the Golden Gate Bridge on a rental bicycle. Besides the main shop on Hyde St, **Blazing Saddles** (Map p40, B2; ☎415-202-8888; www. blazingsaddles.com/san-francisco; 2715 Hyde St; bicycle rental per hour $8-15, per day $32-88, electric bikes per day $48-88; ⊙8am-8pm; 🚼; 🚋Powell-Hyde) has six rental stands around Fisherman's Wharf, and offers electric bikes and 24-hour return service. Reserve online for a 10% discount; rentals includes all extras (helmets, bungee cords, packs etc).

Gold Dust Lounge   BAR

17 🍷 Map p40, C2

The Gold Dust is so beloved by San Franciscans that when it lost its lease on the Union Square building it had occupied since the 1930s, then reopened in 2013 at the Wharf – with the same precarious Victorian brass chandeliers and twangy rockabilly band – the mayor declared it 'Gold Dust Lounge Day.' (☎415-397-1695; www. golddustsf.com; 165 Jefferson St; ⊙9am-2am; 🚌47, 🚋Powell-Mason, Ⓜ F)

Entertainment

Pier 23   LIVE MUSIC

18 ⭐ Map p40, E2

It resembles a surf shack, but this old waterfront restaurant on Pier 23 regularly features R&B, reggae, Latin bands, mellow rock and the occasional jazz pianist. Wander out to the bayside patio to soak in views. The dinner menu features pier-worthy options like batter-fried oysters and whole roasted crab. (☎415-362-5125; www.pier23cafe.com; Pier 23; cover free-$10; ⊙shows 5-7pm Tue, 6-8pm Wed, 7-10pm Thu, 8pm-midnight Fri & Sat, 4-8pm Sun; Ⓜ F)

Buena Vista Cafe

Shopping

Helpers Bazaar   VINTAGE, FASHION

19 🔒 Map p40, A2

Socialite and philanthropist Joy Venturini Bianchi operates this 100%-for-charity boutique, where if you dig, you may find Chanel. If not, there's always costume jewelry and Christmas ornaments. For high-end fashions at secondhand prices, book an appointment at **Helpers House of Couture** (📞415-609-0658, 415-387-3031; 2626 Fulton St; ⊙by appointment; open house one Sunday per month; 🚌5), near GG Park, an entire house packed with top-end couture donated by SF's elite.

(📞415-441-0779; Ghiradelli Square, Plaza Bldg; ⊙10am-9pm Mon-Sat, to 6pm Sun; 🚌19, 30, 47, 49, 🚋Powell-Hyde)

elizabethW   PERFUME

20 🔒 Map p40, A2

Local scent-maker elizabethW supplies the tantalizing aromas of changing seasons without the sweaty brows or frozen toes. 'Sweet Tea' smells like a Georgia porch in summertime; 'Vetiver' like autumn in Maine. For a true SF fragrance, 'Leaves' is as audaciously green as Golden Gate Park in January. (www.elizabethw.com; 900 North Point St; ⊙10am-9pm Mon-Sat, to 8pm Sun; 🚌19, 30, 47, 🚋Powell-Hyde)

Top Sights
Alcatraz

Getting There

⚓ Alcatraz is 1.25 miles across San Francisco Bay from Fisherman's Wharf. Alcatraz Cruises ferries depart from Pier 33 half-hourly from 8:45am to 3:50pm, plus night tours at 5:55pm and 6:30pm; reserve ahead.

Enter a D-Block solitary cell, shut the iron door, and listen carefully: beyond these bars and across the bay, you can hear the murmur of everyday life. Now you understand the peculiar torment of America's most notorious prison – and why inmates risked riptides to escape from Alcatraz. Day visits include captivating audio tours with prisoners and guards recalling cell-house life, while creepy twilight tours are led by park rangers. On the boat back to San Francisco, freedom never felt so good.

Cell block at Alcatraz

Don't Miss

Cell Block

In 1934 America's first military prison became a maximum-security cell block housing most-wanted criminals, from crime boss Al Capone to Soviet spy Morton Sobell. Though Alcatraz was considered escape-proof, in 1962 the Anglin brothers and Frank Morris floated away on a makeshift raft and were never seen again. Their escape plot is showcased on the fascinating cell block tour, which also covers riots, censorship and solitary confinement.

Native American Landmarks

In the 19th century, Alcatraz was a military prison holding Civil War deserters and Native American 'unfriendlies' – including 19 Hopi who refused to send their children to government boarding schools where Hopi language and religion were forbidden. After the prison was closed in 1963, activists petitioned to turn Alcatraz into a Native American study center – but the federal government refused. Native American leaders occupied the island in 1969 in protest, and their 19-month standoff with the FBI is commemorated in a dockside museum and 'This Is Indian Land' graffiti. Public support for the protesters pressured president Richard Nixon to restore Native territory and strengthen self-rule for Native nations.

Nature Trails

After the government regained control of Alcatraz, it became a national park. By 1973 it had already become a major draw for visitors and the namesake birds of Isla de Alcatraces (Isle of the Pelicans). Wear sturdy shoes to explore unpaved trails to the prison laundry area that has become a prime bird-watching zone, and glimpse native plants thriving in the ruins of prison-guard homes.

www.alcatrazcruises.com

day tours adult/child/family $30/18/90, night tours adult/child $37/22

☑ Top Tips

▶ You only need to reserve the ferry to Alcatraz. Book at least three weeks ahead, or a month ahead for twilight tours.

▶ A steep path ascends 130ft from the ferry landing to the cell block, so be prepared to hike or take the twice-hourly tram.

▶ Weather changes fast and it's often windy. Wear layers, long pants and sunblock.

✕ Take a Break

There is no food available on the island – only bottled water, coffee and nuts. Pick up snacks at the Ferry Building before your departure, or hit the snack bar aboard the ferry. Eating is allowed on the island only at the ferry dock.

Top Sights
Exploratorium

Getting There

M Take the F line from the Wharf, downtown or the Castro. Get off at Embarcadero station, and walk four blocks north to Pier 15.

Hear salt sing, stimulate your appetite with color, and try on static-electricity punk hairdos with hands-on exhibits created by MacArthur genius grant winners. Manhattan Project nuclear physicist Frank Oppenheimer founded the Exploratorium in 1969 to explore science, art and human perception – and you can actually simulate '60s flashbacks as you grope barefoot through the Tactile Dome. The thrilling exhibits are matched by the setting: a 9-acre, glass-walled pier jutting over San Francisco Bay.

Exploratorium

Don't Miss

Award-Winning Exhibits

Is there a science to skateboarding? Do toilets really flush counterclockwise in Australia? Find answers to questions you wished you'd learned in school, with 600-plus exhibits that have buttons to push, cranks to ratchet and dials to adjust. Peek into the in-house workshop to see artists and scientists inventing their next extreme science project.

Indoor Galleries

Indoor galleries focus on color, sound, light and motion, and educational photo-ops abound: turn yourself into a human sundial, or get totally trippy in an optical-illusion room. Exploratorium exhibits are purpose-built to excite visitors with possibilities for new inventions, scientific discovery and public service – a fitting tribute to founder Frank Oppenheimer, an atom bomb physicist who was blackballed during the McCarthy era, then later re-emerged as a San Francisco high-school teacher.

Outdoor Gallery

San Francisco's weird science showcase fills a 330,000-sq-ft solar-powered landmark on Pier 15, with vast outdoor portions you can explore for free, 24 hours a day. Listen to the wind play eerie compositions on the 27ft Aeolian harp, see the bay turn upside-down in the Rickshaw Obscura, and spot sensational Over the Water art installations.

Bay Observatory

With assistance from National Oceanic and Atmospheric Admisphoric (NOAA), the Exploratorium's pier is wired with sensors delivering real-time data on weather, wind, tides and the bay. See the data flow at your final stop: Bay Observatory Gallery, a glass-enclosed lookout where sea meets land and sky.

☏ 415-528-4444

www.exploratorium.edu

adult/child $29/19, 6-10pm Thu $15

🕙 10am-5pm Tue-Sun, over 18yr only Thu 6-10pm

☑ Top Tips

▸ Grope your way through the Tactile Dome (reservations and separate $15 ticket required), which challenges you to see with your other four senses.

▸ Step inside the 800-sq-ft Black Box, and you never know what you'll be stumbling into – a field of brainwaves, dancers copying your movements, videos that stop and stare at you.

✗ Take a Break

Get a quick coffee jolt and takeout at entryway **Seismic Joint Café** (🕙 9am-5pm), or splash out on chef Loretta Keller's sustainable fare and cocktails at the Exploratorium's waterfront **Seaglass Restaurant**.

Explore

North Beach & Chinatown

Coffee or tea? East or west? You'll never have to decide in San Francisco, where historic Chinese and Italian neighborhoods are linked by poetry-lined Jack Kerouac Alley. Wander backstreets dotted with pagoda-topped temples and saloons where the Gold Rush, Chinese revolution and the Beat movement started. Rising above it all is Coit Tower, ringed by murals and jealously guarded by parrots.

The Sights in a Day

☀ Start on Grant Ave, lined with pagoda-topped buildings purpose-built in the 1920s by Chinatown merchants to attract curiosity seekers and souvenir shoppers – clearly their plan worked like a charm. Hard to believe this cheerful vintage-neon-signed street was once a notorious red-light district – at least until you see the fascinating displays at the **Chinese Historical Society of America** (p58). Stop by **Tin How Temple** (p59) to admire the altar that miraculously survived the 1906 earthquake, and detour for dim sum at **City View** (p62).

☀ Cross into North Beach via **Jack Kerouac Alley** (pictured left; p59) and **City Lights** (pictured left; p58), San Francisco's free-speech landmark. Espresso at **Caffe Trieste** (p64) turbo-charges your North Beach walking tour, and speeds you up giddy, garden-lined Filbert St Steps to **Coit Tower** (p54).

☽ Brave a Barbary Coast happy-hour crawl from **15 Romolo** (p65) to **Comstock Saloon** (p64) and **Tosca Cafe** (p64). San Franciscans will only excuse you from a final round at **Specs Museum Cafe** (p63) for three reasons: dinner reservations at **Coi** (p60), tickets to **Beach Blanket Babylon** (p66) or shows at **Bimbo's 365 Club** (p66).

◉ Top Sight

Coit Tower & Filbert St Steps (p54)

♥ Best of San Francisco

Fine Dining
Coi (p60)

Bargain Gourmet
Cotogna (p60)

Liguria Bakery (p61)

Z & Y (p61)

Drinks
Caffe Trieste (p64)

Comstock Saloon (p64)

Specs Museum Cafe (p63)

Tosca Cafe (p64)

Shopping
City Lights (p58)

Golden Gate Fortune Cookie Company (p68)

101 Music (p68)

Getting There

🚋 **Cable car** From downtown or the Wharf, take the Powell-Mason line through Chinatown and North Beach. The California St cable car passes through Chinatown.

🚌 **Bus** Key bus routes are 30, 41 and 45.

Top Sights
Coit Tower & Filbert Street Steps

The exclamation point on San Francisco's skyline is Coit Tower, built as a monument to firefighters by eccentric heiress Lillie Hitchcock Coit. This concrete projectile became a lightning rod for controversy for its provocative frescoes of San Francisco during the Great Depression – but no matter your perspective, the tower's viewing platform panoramas are breathtaking. The climb here along wooden Filbert St Steps offers staggering adventure, with wild parrots squawking encouragement.

👁 Map p18

☎ 415-249-0995

Telegraph Hill Blvd

elevator entry (nonresident) adult/child $8/5

🕙 10am-6pm May-Oct, 9am-5pm Nov-Apr

🚌 39

Christopher Columbus statue and Coit Tower

Don't Miss

WPA Murals

Coit Tower's Works Project Administration (WPA) murals show San Franciscans during the Great Depression, gathered at soup kitchens and dock-workers' unions, partying despite Prohibition, and poring over multilingual library books – including Marxist manifestos. These federally funded artworks proved controversial in 1934, and authorities denounced their 26 artists as communist – but San Franciscans embraced Coit Tower's bright, bold murals as beloved city landmarks.

Viewing Platform

After the 20-minute walk uphill to Coit Tower, the wait and admission fee to take the elevator to the top of the tower is well worth it. From the panoramic open-air platform 210ft above San Francisco, you can spot two bridges, cable cars and skyline-defining landmarks.

Filbert Street Steps

In the 19th century a ruthless entrepreneur began quarrying Telegraph Hill and blasting away roads – much to the distress of his neighbors. City Hall eventually stopped the quarrying of Telegraph Hill, but the views of the bay from garden-lined, cliffside Filbert St Steps are still (wait for it) dynamite.

Napier Lane

Along the steep climb from Sansome St up Filbert St Steps toward Coit Tower, stop for a breather along Napier Lane, a wooden boardwalk lined with cottages and gardens where wild parrots have flocked for decades.

☑ Top Tips

▶ To see seven murals hidden inside Coit Tower's stairwell, take the free, docent-led tour at 11am on Wednesdays and Saturdays.

▶ For a bird's-eye view of San Francisco, don't miss the award-winning 2005 documentary *The Wild Parrots of Telegraph Hill*.

▶ Bus 39 heads to Coit Tower from Fisherman's Wharf – but for scenic walks, take Filbert St or Greenwich St Steps.

✗ Take a Break

Pick up fresh focaccia at Liguria Bakery (p61) to share with parrots (or not) atop Telegraph Hill.

For protein-powered hikes, get Molinari (p63) salami sandwiches.

Montgomery St

Columbus Ave

⊗ 30

🏛 34

Chinese
Culture
Center

4 ◉

Mark Twain St

Commercial St

Spring St

Belden Pl

Kearny St

Kearny St

12 ⊗

Bush St

Claude La

Sutter St

Washington St

Portsmouth
Square

St Mary's
Square

Pine St

25 ◉

Harlan Pl

20 ◉

Jackson St

⊗ ⊗
11 15

CHINATOWN

Sacramento St

California St

California St

Quincy St

Grant Ave

Kearny St

Beckett St

23 ◉

Clay St

36 ◉◉◉
35

Grant Ave

Sacramento St

Grant Ave

31 ◉

Tin How
Temple

6 ◉

Waverly Pl

Stockton St

Stockton St

Chinese Historical
Society of America

2 ◉

Joice St

Powell St

Stone St

Powell St

Wetmore St

John St

Mason St

Mason St

Mason St

Sproule La

Cushman
St

California St

Pine St

Bush St

Auburn St

Huntington
Park

Taylor St

Bernard St

Pacific Ave

Taylor St

Washington St

Jackson St

Clay St

Pleasant St

Sacramento St

Taylor St

Jones St

NOB
HILL

Jones St

Broadway Tunnel

Priest St

Reed St

Sights

City Lights
CULTURAL CENTER, LANDMARK

1 ◎ Map p56, D4

Free speech and free spirits have flourished at City Lights since 1957, when founder and poet Lawrence Ferlinghetti and manager Shigeyoshi Murao won a landmark ruling defending their right to publish Allen Ginsberg's magnificent epic poem 'Howl.' Celebrate your right to read freely in the sunny upstairs Poetry Room, with its piles of freshly published verse and designated Poet's Chair. (☑415-362-8193; www.citylights.com; 261 Columbus Ave; ◎10am-midnight; ⑭; ◱8, 10, 12, 30, 41, 45, 🚃Powell-Mason, Powell-Hyde)

Chinese Historical Society of America
MUSEUM

2 ◎ Map p56, C6

Picture what it was like to be Chinese in America during the Gold Rush, transcontinental railroad construction or Beat heyday in this 1932 landmark, built as Chinatown's YWCA by Julia Morgan (chief architect of Hearst Castle). CHSA historians unearth fascinating artifacts, such as 1920s silk *qipao* dresses worn by socialites from Shanghai to San Francisco. Exhibits reveal once-popular views of Chinatown, including the sensationalist opium den exhibit at San Francisco's 1915 Panama-Pacific International Expo, inviting fairgoers to 'Go Slumming' in Chinatown. (CHSA; ☑415-391-1188; www.chsa.org; 965 Clay St; admission free; ◎noon-5pm Tue-Fri, 11am-4pm Sat; ◱1, 8, 30, 45, 🚃California St, Powell-Mason, Mason-Hyde)

Beat Museum
MUSEUM

3 ◎ Map p56, D4

The closest you can get to the complete Beat experience without breaking a law. The 1000+ artifacts in this museum's literary ephemera collection include the sublime (the banned edition of Ginsberg's *Howl*) and the ridiculous (those Kerouac bobble-head dolls are definite head-shakers). Downstairs, watch Beat-era films in ramshackle theater seats redolent with the odors of literary giants, pets and pot. Upstairs, pay respects at shrines to individual Beat writers. Guided two-hour walking tours cover the museum, Beat history and literary alleys. (☑1-800-537-6822; www.kerouac.com; 540 Broadway; adult/student $8/5; walking tour $25; ◎museum 10am-7pm; walking tour 2-4pm Mon, Wed & Sat; ◱8, 10, 12, 30, 41, 45, 🚃Powell-Mason)

Chinese Culture Center
ART GALLERY

4 ◎ Map p56, E5

You can see all the way to China from the Hilton's 3rd floor inside this cultural center, which hosts exhibits ranging from showcases of China's leading ink-brush-painters to XianRui ('fresharp') cutting-edge installations, recently including videos exploring generation gaps. In odd-numbered years, don't miss Present Tense Biennial, where 30-plus Bay Area artists present personal takes on Chinese culture. Check the center's online schedule for upcoming concerts, hands-on arts workshops for adults and children, Mandarin classes and genealogy services. (☎415-986-1822; www.c-c-c.org; 3rd fl, Hilton Hotel, 750 Kearny St; suggested donation $5; ⏲during exhibitions 10am-4pm Tue-Sat; ♿; 🚌1, 8, 10, 12, 30, 41, 45, 🚋California St, Powell-Mason, Powell-Hyde)

Jack Kerouac Alley STREET

5 ◉ Map p56, D4

'The air was soft, the stars so fine, the promise of every cobbled alley so great...' This ode by the *On the Road* and *The Dharma Bums* author is embedded in his namesake alley, a fittingly poetic and slightly seedy shortcut between Chinatown and North Beach via Kerouac haunts City Lights and Vesuvio – Kerouac took literature, Buddhism and beer seriously. (btwn Grant & Columbus Aves; 🚌8, 10, 12, 30, 41, 45, 🚋Powell-Mason)

Tin How Temple TEMPLE

6 ◉ Map p56, D6

There was no place to go but up in Chinatown in the 19th century, when laws restricted where Chinese San Franciscans could live and work. Atop barber shops, laundries and diners lining Waverly Place, you'll spot lantern-festooned temple balconies. Tin How Temple was built in 1852; its

VISIONS OF AMERICA / GETTY IMAGES ©

Chinatown

altar miraculously survived the 1906 earthquake. To pay your respects, follow sandalwood incense aromas up three flights of stairs. Entry is free, but offerings customary for temple upkeep. No photography is allowed inside. (Tien Hau Temple; 125 Waverly Place; donation customary; ⏲10am-4pm, except holidays; 🚌1, 8, 30, 45, 🚋California St, Powell-Mason, Powell-Hyde)

Saints Peter & Paul Cathedral and Washington Square Park CHURCH

7 ◉ Map p56, C2

Wedding-cake cravings are inspired by this frosted-white, triple-layer 1924 **cathedral** (☎415-421-0809; www. sspeterpaulsf.org/church; 666 Filbert St;

⏱7:30am-12:30pm Mon-Fri, to 5pm Sat & Sun; 🚌8,30, 39, 41, 45, 🚋Powell-Mason) where Joe DiMaggio and Marilyn Monroe posed for wedding photos (as divorcees, they were denied a church wedding here). The cathedral faces Washington Sq, where grandmothers practice tai chi by the 1897 statue of Ben Franklin, donated by an eccentric dentist who made fortunes in gold teeth. (Columbus Ave & Union St; 🚌39, 🚋Powell-Mason)

Eating

Coi

CALIFORNIAN $$$

8 Map p56, E4

Chef Daniel Patterson's restlessly imaginative 12-course tasting menu is like licking the California coastline:

satiny Meyer-lemon gelee melts onto oysters, nutty wild morels hug blush-pink trout, California sturgeon caviar crowns velvety smoked farm-egg yolk. Bright, only-in-California flavors deserve adventurous wine pairings ($105; generous enough for two). Book your 'ticket' online, or chance a walk-in ($20 more per person); 20% service and tax added. (📞415-393-9000; www. coirestaurant.com; 373 Broadway; set menu $195; ⏱5:30-10pm Tue-Sat; 🅿; 🚌8,10,12, 30, 41, 45, 🚋Powell-Mason)

Cotogna

ITALIAN $$

9 Map p56, E4

Chef-owner Michael Tusk is racking up James Beard Awards for best chef, and you'll discover why: he balances

---

Understand
Chinatown Alleyways

Forty-one historic alleyways packed into Chinatown's 22 blocks have seen it all since 1849: Gold Rushes and revolution, incense and opium, fire and icy receptions. Though Chinese miners were among the first to arrive in San Francisco's Gold Rush, 1870s Asian Exclusion laws restricted Chinese immigration, employment and housing. Anti-Chinese laws served local magnates looking for cheap labor to do dangerous work dynamiting tunnels for the first cross-country railroad. Chinatown's white landlords also profited handsomely from basement opium dens along Duncombe Alley and brothels lining Ross Alley.

When the 1906 earthquake and fire devastated Chinatown, developers convinced the city to relocate Chinatown outside city limits. But the Chinese consulate and rifle-toting Chinatown merchants defied the expulsion order, marching back into Chinatown. To attract legitimate tourist trade, Chinatown merchants rebuilt in a signature pagoda-topped 'Chinatown deco' style. Today Chinatown's historic alleys are calm – you can hear the clatter of mahjong tiles at 36 Spofford Alley, where Sun Yat-sen once plotted revolution.

Understand
The Beat Generation

US armed services personnel dismissed in WWII for disobeying orders, homosexuality and other 'subversive' behavior were discharged in San Francisco, as though that would teach them a lesson. Instead, they found themselves at home in nonconformist North Beach. So during McCarthyism, rebels and romantics headed for San Francisco – including Jack Kerouac. By the time *On the Road* was published in 1957, the fellow writers, artists and dreamers Kerouac affectionately called 'the mad ones' and the press derisively dubbed 'beatniks' were San Francisco regulars.

Police fined 'beatnik chicks' for wearing sandals, and were taunted in verse by African American street-corner prophet Bob Kaufman (North Beach's Bob Kaufman Alley (p164), off Grant Ave near Filbert St, duly honors him). Poet Lawrence Ferlinghetti and manager Shigeyoshi Murao of City Lights (p58) bookstore fought the law and won, after their arrest for 'willfully and lewdly' publishing Allen Ginsberg's 'Howl'. The kindred Beat spirits 'Howl' describes as 'angel-headed hipsters burning for the ancient heavenly connection' made more waves, art and love than money, upending 1950s social-climbing conventions – and making way for 1960s counterculture.

a few pristine flavors in rustic pastas, woodfired pizzas and authentic Florentine steak. Reserve ahead or plan to eat late (2pm to 5pm) to score the bargain $28 prix-fixe lunch. On the excellent wine list all bottles cost $50, including hard-to-find Italian cult wines. (☑415-775-8508; www.cotognasf.com; 490 Pacific Ave; mains $17-38; ☺11:30am-10:30pm Mon-Thu, to 11pm Fri & Sat, 5-9:30pm Sun; ☝; ☐10, 12)

Liguria Bakery   BAKERY $
10 ☒ Map p56, C2

Bleary-eyed art students and Italian grandmothers are in line by 8am for cinnamon-raisin focaccia hot out of the 100-year-old oven, leaving 9am

dawdlers a choice of tomato or classic rosemary/garlic and 11am stragglers out of luck. Take yours in wax paper or boxed for picnics – but don't kid yourself that you're going to save some for later. Cash only. (☑415-421-3786; 1700 Stockton St; focaccia $4-5; ☺8am-1pm Tue-Fri, from 7am Sat; ☝ ☗; ☐8, 30, 39, 41, 45, ☐Powell-Mason)

Z & Y   CHINESE $$
11 ☒ Map p56, D5

Graduate from ho-hum sweet-and-sour and middling *mu-shu* to sensational Szechuan dishes that go down in a blaze of glory. Warm up with spicy pork dumplings and heat-blistered string beans, take on the house-made *tantan* noodles with pea-nut-chili sauce, and leave lips buzzing with fish poached in flaming chili oil and buried under red Szechuan chili-peppers. Go early; it's worth the wait. (☑415-981-8988; www.zandyrestaurant.com; 655 Jackson St; mains $9-20; ⏱11am-10pm Mon-Thu, to 11pm Fri-Sun; 🚌8, 10,12,30,45, 🚋Powell-Mason, Powell-Hyde)

City View
CHINESE $

14 🍴 Map p56, E6

Take your seat in the sunny dining room and your pick from carts loaded with delicate shrimp and leek dump-lings, garlicky Chinese broccoli, tangy spare ribs, coconut-dusted custard tarts and other tantalizing dim sum. Arrive before the midday lunch rush, so you can nab seats in the sunny upstairs room and get first dibs from passing carts. (☑415-398-2838; http://cityviewdimsum.com; 662 Commercial St; dishes $3-8; ⏱11am-2:30pm Mon-Fri, from 10am Sat & Sun; 🚼; 🚌1,8, 10, 12, 30, 45, 🚋California St)

Ristorante Ideale
ITALIAN $$

13 🍴 Map p56, D3

Other North Beach restaurants fake Italian accents, but this trattoria has Italians in the kitchen, on the floor and at the table. Roman chef-owner Maurizio Bruschi serves authentic, al dente *bucatini ammatriciana* (tube pasta with tomato-pecorino sauce and house-cured pancetta) and ravioli and gnocchi handmade in-house ('of course!'). Ask Tuscan staff to recom-

mend well-priced wine and everyone goes home happy. (☑415-391-4129; www.idealerestaurant.com; 1309 Grant Ave; pasta $16-20; ⏱5:30-10:30pm Mon-Thu, to 11pm Fri & Sat, 5-10pm Sun; 🚌8, 10, 12, 30, 41, 45, 🚋Powell-Mason)

Cinecittà
PIZZA $$

14 🍴 Map p56, C3

Follow tantalizing aromas into this tiny hotspot for thin-crust Roman pizza, made from scratch and served with sass by Roman owner Romina. Local loyalties are divided between the Roman Travestere (fresh moz-zarella, arugula and prosciutto) and Neapolitan O Sole Mio (capers, olives, mozzarella and anchovies). Local brews are on tap, house wine is $5 from 4pm to 7pm, and Romina's tiramisu is San Francisco's best. (☑415-291-8830; www.cinecittarestaurant.com; 663 Union St; pizza $12-15; ⏱noon-10pm Sun-Thu, to 11pm Fri & Sat; 🍴🚼; 🚌8X, 30, 39, 41, 45, 🚋Powell-Mason)

Great Eastern Restaurant
CHINESE, DIM SUM $$

15 🍴 Map p56, D5

Eat your way across China, from northern Peking duck to southern pan-fried shrimp and Cantonese chive dumplings. President Obama stopped by Great Eastern for takeout and weekend dim sum throngs around noon may make you wish for your own secret-service escort – call ahead for reservations or come around 1pm as dim sum brunch crowds stagger

out satisfied. (☎415-986-2500; http://
greateasternrestaurant.net; 649 Jackson
St; mains $8-20; ⊗10am-11pm Mon-Fri,
from 9am Sat & Sun; 🚼; 🚌8,10,12,30,45,
🚋Powell-Mason, Powell-Hyde)

Molinari   DELI $

16 🍴 Map p56, D4

Grab a number and a crusty roll, and
when your number rolls around, wise-
cracking deli staff in paper hats will
stuff it with translucent sheets of *prosciutto di Parma,* milky buffalo mozzarella, tender marinated artichokes
or slabs of the legendary house-cured
salami. Enjoy yours hot from the
panini press at sidewalk tables or in
Washington Square. (☎415-421-2337;
www.molinarisalame.com; 373 Columbus Ave;
sandwiches $10-12.50; ⊗9am-6pm Mon-Fri,
to 5:30pm Sat, 10am-4pm Sun; 🚌8,10,12 30,
39, 41, 45, 🚋Powell-Mason)

Golden Boy   PIZZA $

17 🍴 Map p56, D3

Looking for the ultimate slice post-
bar-crawl and morning-after brunch?
Here you're golden. Second-generation
Sodini family pizza-slingers make theirs
Genovese-style with focaccia crust, hit-
ting that mystical mean between chewy
and crunchy with the ideal amount of
olive oil. Go for Genovese toppings like
clam/garlic or pesto, and bliss out with
hot slices and draft beer at the tin-shed
counter. (☎415-982-9738; www.golden
boypizza.com; 542 Green St; slice $2.75-3.75;
⊗11:30am-11:30pm Sun-Thu, to 2:30am Fri &
Sat; 🚌8,30,39,41,45, 🚋Powell-Mason)

Molinari

Drinking

Specs Museum Cafe   BAR

18 🍺 Map p56, D4

What do you do with a drunken
sailor? Here's your answer. The walls
are plastered with merchant-marine
mementos, and you'll be plastered too
if you try to keep up with the salty
old-timers holding court in back.
Surrounded by nautical memorabilia,
your order is obvious: pitcher of Anchor Steam, coming right up. (☎415-
421-4112; 12 William Saroyan Pl; ⊗5pm-2am;
🚌8, 10, 12, 30, 41, 45, 🚋Powell-Mason)

Caffe Trieste

CAFÉ

19 Map p56, D4

Poetry on bathroom walls, opera on the jukebox, live accordion jams and sightings of Beat poet laureate Lawrence Ferlinghetti: this is North Beach at its best, since the 1950s. Linger over legendary espresso and scribble your screenplay under the Sardinian fishing mural just as young Francis Ford Coppola did. Perhaps you've heard of the movie: *The Godfather*. Cash only. (☏ 415-392-6739; www.caffetrieste.com; 601 Vallejo St; ⏱ 6:30am-10pm Sun-Thu, to 11pm Fri & Sat; 📶; 🚌 8, 10, 12, 30, 41, 45)

Top Tip

Parking Luck

You'd be lucky to find parking anywhere near Chinatown or North Beach, but a free space in the **Good Luck Parking Garage** (Map p56, C4; 735 Vallejo St; 🚌 10, 12, 30, 41, 45, 🚋 Powell-Mason) brings double happiness. Each parking spot offers fortune-cookie wisdom stenciled onto the asphalt: 'You have already found your true love. Stop looking.' These car-locating omens are brought to you by West Coast artists Harrell Fletcher and Jon Rubin, who also gathered the photographs of local residents' Chinese and Italian ancestors that grace the entry in heraldic emblems.

Comstock Saloon

BAR

20 Map p56, D5

Relieving yourself in the marble trough below the bar is no longer advisable, but otherwise this 1907 Victorian saloon revives the Barbary Coast's glory days. Get the authentic Pisco Punch or martini-precursor Martinez (gin, vermouth, bitters, maraschino liqueur). Reserve booths or back-parlor seating, so you can hear dates when ragtime-jazz bands play. Call it dinner with pot pie and buckets of shrimp. (☏ 415-617-0071; www.comstocksaloon.com; 155 Columbus Ave; ⏱ noon-2am Mon-Fri, 4pm-2am Sat, 4pm-midnight Sun; 🚌 8, 10, 12, 30, 45, 🚋 Powell-Mason)

Tosca Cafe

BAR

21 Map p56, D4

When this historic North Beach speakeasy was nearly evicted in 2012, devotees like Sean Penn, Bobby DeNiro and Johnny Depp rallied, and New York star-chef April Bloomfield took over. Now 1930s murals and red leather banquettes are restored, and the revived kitchen serves rustic Italian fare (get the meatballs). Jukebox opera and spiked house cappuccino here deserve SF landmark status. Reservations essential. (☏ 415-986-9651; www.toscacafesf.com; 242 Columbus Ave; ⏱ 5pm-2am; 🚌 8, 10, 12, 30, 41, 45, 🚋 Powell-Mason)

15 Romolo
BAR

22 Map p56, D4

Strap on your spurs: it's gonna be a wild western night at this back-alley Basque saloon squeezed between burlesque joints. The strong survive the Suckerpunch, a knockout potion of bourbon, sherry, hibiscus, lemon and Basque bitters – but everyone falls for Frida Kahlo, with mezcal, chartreuse, lavender and lemon. Bask in $7 Basque Picon punch from 5pm to 7:30pm happy hours. (☏415-398-1359; www.15romolo.com; 15 Romolo Pl; ⏰5pm-2am Mon-Fri, from 11:30am Sat & Sun; ☒8, 10, 12, 30, 41, 45, ☒Powell-Mason)

Li Po
BAR

23 Map p56, D5

Beat a hasty retreat to red vinyl booths where Allen Ginsberg and Jack Kerouac debated the meaning of life under a golden Buddha. Enter the 1937 faux-grotto doorway and dodge red lanterns to place your order: Tsing Tao beer or sweet, sneaky-strong Chinese mai tai made with *baijiu* (rice liquor). Bathrooms and random DJ appearances are in the basement. Cash only. (☏415-982-0072; www.lipolounge.com; 916 Grant Ave; ⏰2pm-2am; ☒8, 30, 45, ☒Powell-Mason, Powell-Hyde)

Réveille
CAFÉ

24 Map p56, E4

If this sunny flatiron storefront doesn't instantly lighten your mood, cappuccino with a foam-art heart will.

Local Life
Red Blossom Tea Company

Several Grant Ave tea importers offer free samples, but the hard sell may begin before you finish sipping. For more relaxed, enlightening tea-tasting, **Red Blossom Tea Company** (Map p56, D6; ☏415-395-0868; www.redblossomtea.com; 831 Grant Ave; ⏰10am-6:30pm Mon-Sat, to 6pm Sun; ☒1, 10, 12, 30, 35, 41, ☒Powell-Mason, Powell-Hyde, California St) offers half-hour courses with four to five tastings and preparation tips to maximize flavor ($30 for up to four participants; drop-in weekdays, reserve ahead weekends).

Réveille's coffee is like San Francisco on a good day: nutty and uplifting, without a trace of bitterness. Check the circular marble counter for just-baked chocolate-chip cookies and sticky buns. No wi-fi makes for easy conversation and sidewalk-facing counters offer some of SF's best people-watching. (☏415-789-6258; http://reveillecoffee.com; 200 Columbus Ave; ⏰7am-6pm Mon-Fri, from 8am Sat, 8am-5pm Sun; ☒8, 10, 12, 30, 41, 45, ☒Powell-Mason)

PlenTea
TEAHOUSE

25 Map p56, E7

Chinatown's latest, greatest import is Taiwanese bubble tea, milky iced tea polka-dotted with *boba* (chewy, gently sweet tapioca pearls). PlenTea fills vintage milk bottles with just-brewed bubble tea in your choice of flavors: green, black, oolong, Thai, or any of the above plus fresh mango, peach or strawberry. For only-in-SF flavor, try extra-rich crema tea with oolong and sea-salt cream. (☎415-757-0223; www.plenteasf.com; 341 Kearny St; ⏱11am-11pm; 🚇1,8,30,45, 🚋California St)

Vesuvio BAR

26 🚇 Map p56, D4

Guy walks into a bar, roars and leaves. Without missing a beat, the bartender says to the next customer, 'Welcome to Vesuvio, honey – what can I get you?' Jack Kerouac blew off Henry Miller to go on a bender here, and after joining neighborhood characters on the stained-glass mezzanine for microbrews or Kerouacs (rum, tequila and OJ), you'll get why. (☎415-362-3370; www.vesuvio.com; 255 Columbus Ave; ⏱6am-2am; 🚇8, 10, 12, 30, 41, 45, 🚋Powell-Mason)

Entertainment

Beach Blanket Babylon CABARET

27 ⭐ Map p56, C3

Snow White searches for Prince Charming in San Francisco: what could possibly go wrong? The Disney-spoof musical-comedy cabaret has been running since 1974, but topical jokes keep it outrageous and wigs big as parade floats are gasp-worthy. Spectators must be over 21 to handle racy humor, except at cleverly sanitized Sunday matinees. Reservations

essential; arrive one hour early for the best seats. (BBB; ☎415-421-4222; www.beachblanketbabylon.com; 678 Green St; tickets $25-100; ⏱shows 8pm Wed, Thu & Fri, 6:30pm & 9:30pm Sat, 2pm & 5pm Sun; 🚇8,30,39,41,45, 🚋Powell-Mason)

Cobb's Comedy Club COMEDY

28 ⭐ Map p56, A1

There's no room to be shy at Cobb's, where bumper-to-bumper tables make an intimate (and vulnerable) audience. The venue is known for launching local talent and giving big-name acts from Louis CK to Kevin Smith a place to try risky new material. Check the website for shows and showcases like Really Funny Comedians (Who Happen to Be Women). (☎415-928-4320; www.cobbs comedyclub.com; 915 Columbus Ave; tickets $13-45, plus 2-drink minimum; ⏱showtimes vary; 🚇8, 30, 39, 41, 45, 🚋Powell-Mason)

Bimbo's 365 Club LIVE MUSIC

29 ⭐ Map p56, A1

Get your kicks at this vintage speakeasy with stiff drinks, bawdy 1951 bar murals, parquet dance floor for high-stepping like Rita Hayworth (she was in the chorus line here), and intimate live shows by the likes of Beck, Pinback, English Beat and Bebel Gilberto. Bring change to tip the ladies' powder room attendant – this is a classy joint. Two-drink minimum; cash only. (☎415-474-0365; www.bimbos365club.com; 1025 Columbus Ave; tickets from $20; ⏱box office 10am-4pm, showtimes vary; 🚇8, 30, 39, 41, 45, 🚋Powell-Mason)

PETER DASILVA / CORBIS ©

Bimbo's 365 Club

Understand
The Barbary Coast

By 1854 San Francisco's harbor near Portsmouth Sq was filling with rotting ships abandoned by crews with Gold Rush fever. Here on the ragged piers of the 'Barbary Coast,' a buck might procure whiskey, opium or a woman's company at 500 saloons, 20 theaters and numerous brothels – but buyer beware. Saloon owners like Shanghai Kelly and notorious madam Miss Piggot would ply new arrivals with booze, knock them out with drugs or billy-clubs, and deliver them to sea captains in need of crews. At the gaming tables, luck literally was a lady: women card dealers dealt winning hands to those who engaged their back-room services.

Prohibition and California's 1913 Red Light Abatement Act drove the Barbary Coast's illicit action underground, but it never really went away. US obscenity laws were defied post-WWII in anything-goes North Beach clubs near Broadway and Columbus, where burlesque dancer Carol Doda went topless and comedian Lenny Bruce dropped F-bombs. Today San Francisco is undergoing a Barbary Coast saloon revival, with potent 19th-century-style cocktails served by apparently harmless bartenders – just don't forget to tip.

Top Tip

Chinatown Walks

Local-led, kid-friendly **Chinatown Heritage Walking Tours** (☏415-986-1822; www.c-c-c.org; tours depart Chinese Cultural Center, 3rd fl, Hilton Hotel, 750 Kearny St; group walking tour adult/student $25-30/15-20, private walking tour (1-4 people) $60; ☉tours 10am, noon & 2pm Tue-Sat; ☐1,8,10,12,30,41,45, ☐California, Powell-Mason, Powell-Hyde) guide visitors through the living history of Chinatown in two hours. Themes include The Tale of Two Chinatowns, covering Chinatown's daily life and cultural influence, and From Dynasty to Democracy, which explores Chinatown's role in the US civil rights movement and international human rights struggles. All proceeds support the Chinese Culture Center; bookings can be made online or by phone.

Chinatown Alleyway Tours (☏415-984-1478; www.chinatownalleywaytours.org; adult/student $26/16; ☉11am Sat; ☂; ☐1, 8, 10, 41) offers two-hour Chinatown backstreet walks led by local teens; proceeds support the nonprofit Chinatown Community Development Center.

Doc's Lab   LIVE MUSIC, COMEDY

30 ⭐ Map p56, E5

Social experiments begin in this subterranean venue, where potent drinks are concocted with mad-scientist beakers and the daring bill upholds North Beach traditions of experimental jazz, out-there comedy, boom-boom burlesque and anything-goes Americana. Doc's Lab occupies the space left by the legendary Purple Onion, home of breakout performances from Maya Angelou to Zach Galifianakis – and fills the void. (☏415-649-6191; www.docslabsf.com; 124 Columbus Ave; admission free-$20; ☉showtimes vary, see website; ☐8,10,12,30,41,45, ☐Powell-Mason)

Shopping

Golden Gate Fortune Cookie Company   FOOD & DRINK

31 🔒 Map p56, D5

Make a fortune in San Francisco at this bakery, where cookies are stamped from vintage presses and folded while hot – much as they were in 1909, when fortune cookies were invented for San Francisco's Japanese Tea Garden (p153). Write your own wise words for custom cookies (50¢ each) or get bags of regular or risqué cookies. Cash only; 50¢ tip per photo. (☏415-781-3956; 56 Ross Alley; ☉8am-6pm; ☐8,30, 45, ☐Powell-Mason, Powell-Hyde)

101 Music   MUSIC

32 🔒 Map p56, D3

You'll have to bend over those bins to let DJs and hardcore collectors pass (and, hey, wasn't that Tom Waits?!), but among the $8–25 discs are obscure releases (*Songs for Greek Lovers*) and original recordings by Nina Simone, Janis Joplin and San

Francisco's own anthem-rockers, Journey. At the sister shop (513 Green St), don't bonk your head on vintage Les Pauls. (☎415-392-6369; 1414 Grant Ave; ◷10am-8pm Mon-Sat, from noon Sun; 🚌8, 30, 39, 41, 45, 🚋Powell-Mason)

Aria
ANTIQUES, COLLECTIBLES

33 🔒 Map p56, D2

Find inspiration for your own North Beach epic poem on Aria's weathered wood counters, piled with anatomical drawings of starfish, castle keys lost in gutters a century ago, rusty numbers pried from French village walls and 19th-century letters still in their wax-sealed envelopes. Hours are erratic whenever owner-chief scavenger Bill Haskell is treasure-hunting abroad, so call ahead. (☎415-433-0219; 1522 Grant Ave; ◷11am-6pm Mon-Sat; 🚌8, 30, 39, 41, 45, 🚋Powell-Mason)

Eden & Eden
GIFTS, ACCESSORIES

34 🔒 Map p56, E5

Detour from reality at Eden & Eden, a Dadaist design boutique where necklaces declare you psychic, galaxies twinkle on '70s silk dresses, shaggy tea cozies make teapots look bearded, and a stuffed mouse in a white wig calls himself Andy Warhol. Prices are surprisingly down to earth for far-out, limited-edition and repurposed-vintage finds from local and international designers. (www.edenandeden.com; 560 Jackson St; ◷10am-7pm Mon-Fri, to 6pm Sat; 🚌8,10,12,41)

Chinatown Kite Shop
GIFTS

35 🔒 Map p56, D6

Be the star of Crissy Field and wow any kids in your life with a fierce 9ft-long flying dragon, a pirate-worthy wild parrot (SF's city bird), surreal floating legs or a flying panda that looks understandably stunned. Pick up a two-person, papier-mâché lion dance costume and invite a date to bust ferocious moves with you next lunar new year. (☎415-989-5182; www. chinatownkite.com; 717 Grant Ave; ◷10am-8pm; 🚼; 🚌1, 10, 12, 30, 35, 41, 🚋Powell-Hyde, Powell-Mason, California St)

Far East Flea Market
GIFTS

36 🔒 Map p56, D6

The shopping equivalent of crack, this bottomless store is dangerously cheap and certain to make you giddy and delusional. Of course you can get that $8.99 samurai sword through airport security! There's no such thing as too many bath toys, bobble-heads and Chia Pets! Step away from the $1 Golden Gate Bridge snow globes while there's still time... (☎415-989-8588; 729 Grant Ave; ◷10am-9:30pm; 🚌1, 10, 12, 30, 35, 41, 🚋Powell-Mason, Powell-Hyde, California St)

Local Life
Russian Hill & Nob Hill Secrets

Getting There

Nob Hill stands between downtown and Chinatown; Russian Hill abuts Fisherman's Wharf and North Beach.

🚋 California St, Powell-Hyde and Powell-Mason cable cars cover steep hillside streets.

Cloud nine can't compare to the upper reaches of Nob Hill and Russian Hill, where hilltop gardens, literary landmarks and divine views await discovery up flower-lined stairway walks. If the climb and the sights don't leave you completely weak in the knees, try staggering back downhill after a couple of Nob Hill cocktails. Now you understand why San Francisco invented cable cars.

❶ Conquer Vallejo Street Steps

Begin your ascent of Russian Hill from North Beach, where **Vallejo St Steps** rise toward Jones St past Zen gardens and flower-framed apartments. When fog blows, listen for whooshing in the treetops and the irregular music of wind chimes. Stop to catch your breath, then turn around and lose it again with seagull's-eye views of the Bay Bridge.

❷ Wax Poetic at Ina Coolbrith Park

On San Francisco's literary scene, all roads eventually lead to Ina Coolbrith, California's first poet laureate; colleague of Mark Twain and Ansel Adams; mentor to Jack London, Isadora Duncan and Charlotte Perkins Gilman. One association she kept secret: her uncle was Mormon prophet Joseph Smith. **Ina Coolbrith Park** (Vallejo & Taylor Sts; 🚌10, 12, 🚋Powell-Mason) is a fitting honor: secret and romantic, with exclamation-inspiring vistas.

❸ Discover Mysterious Macondray Lane

The scenic route down from Ina Coolbrith Park – via steep stairs, past gravity-defying wooden cottages – is so charming, it could be a scene from a novel. And so it is: Armistead Maupin used **Macondray Lane** (btwn Jones & Leavenworth Sts; 🚌41, 45, 🚋Powell-Mason, Powell-Hyde) as the model for Barbary Lane in his *Tales of the City* mysteries.

❹ Spot Kerouac's Love Shack

This **modest house** (29 Russell St; 🚌41, 45, 🚋Powell-Hyde) on a quiet alley witnessed drama in 1951–52, when Jack Kerouac shacked up with Neal and Carolyn Cassady to pound out his 120ft-long scroll draft of *On the Road*. Jack and Carolyn became lovers at Neal's suggestion, but Carolyn frequently kicked them both out. Neal was allowed back for the birth of John Allen Cassady (named for Jack and Allen Ginsberg).

❺ Find Unexpected Graces at Grace Cathedral

Hop the Powell-Hyde cable car to Nob Hill's crest, graced by Gothic **Grace Cathedral** (📞415-749-6300; 1100 California St; 🕗8am-6pm Mon-Sat, to 7pm Sun, services 8:30am, 11am, 6pm Sun; 🚌1, 🚋California St). Labyrinths outside and indoors set a contemplative mood, while stained-glass windows celebrate religious dissidents and scientists. Grace's commitment to social issues is embodied in Keith Haring's cartoon-angel altarpiece for AIDS Memorial Chapel.

❻ Drink up a Storm at the Tonga Room

Tonight's weather: partly foggy, with 100% chance of tropical rainstorms every 20 minutes inside the **Tonga Room** (📞415-772-5278; Fairmont San Francisco, 950 Mason St; cover $5-7; 🕗5:30-11:30pm Sun, Wed & Thu, 5pm-12:30am Fri & Sat; 🚌1, 🚋California St, Powell-Mason, Powell-Hyde). Don't worry, you'll stay dry in your grass hut – the rain only falls on the indoor pool, where cover bands play on an island after 8pm.

Explore

Downtown & SoMa

Get to know SF from the inside out, from art museums to farmers markets. Discover fine dining that's unfussy yet fabulous, and find out why some cocktails are worth double digits – and sleep is over-rated. Social-media headquarters rub shoulders with drag venues South of Market St (SoMa), and after 10pm, everyone gets down and dirty on the dance floor.

The Sights in a Day

☀ Graze your way through the **Ferry Building** (pictured left; p74) and its year-round, thrice-weekly farmers market to a fortifying bayside brunch at **Boulette's Larder** (p75). Now you're ready for your SoMa art binge: the **Contemporary Jewish Museum** (p82) for think-pieces inside a Libeskind landmark and the **California Historical Society Museum** (p83) and **Museum of the African Diaspora** (p82) for local memories and global context.

☀ Window-shop around **Union Square** (p90), then hop the **Powell-Hyde cable car** (p76) to giddy Golden Gate Bridge views. Return downtown for the happy hour of your choice: oysters and bubbly at **Hog Island Oyster Company** (p75), Prohibition-pedigreed cocktails at **Bar Agricole** (p87), pints at **Irish Bank** (p89) or knockout Pisco Punch at **Rickhouse** (p87).

☾ Plan the rest of your night around a SoMa club crawl, **ACT** (p90) theater tickets, reservations at **Benu** (p84) or drag extravaganzas at **Oasis** (p91).

 Top Sights

Ferry Building (p74)

Cable Cars (p76)

 Best of San Francisco

Museums

Contemporary Jewish Museum (p82)

California Historical Society Museum (p83)

SFMOMA (p84)

LGBT

BeatBox (p88)

Eagle Tavern (p88)

EndUp (p90)

Stud (p91)

Oasis (p91)

DNA Lounge (p92)

Cat Club (p88)

Madame S & Mr S Leather (p95)

Getting There

Ⓜ Ⓑ Streetcars and BART subways run along Market St.

🚌 **Bus** East–west buses include 14 Mission and 47 Harrison (to Fisherman's Wharf); north–south include 27 Bryant (Mission to Russian Hill) and 19 Polk.

🚗 **Car** Garage at Mission & 5th Sts.

Top Sights
Ferry Building

Slackers have the right idea at this transport hub turned gourmet emporium, where no one's in a hurry to leave. Boat traffic dwindled since the grand hall was built in 1898, so in 2003 the city converted the Ferry Building into a monumental tribute to the Bay Area's innovative, sustainable food, garnished with California's most famous farmers market. Further reasons to miss that ferry await indoors: James Beard Award–winning restaurants, artisan chocolates, and foodie boutiques to bring inspiration home.

Map p80, H2

415-983-8030

Market St & the Embarcadero

10am-6pm Mon-Fri, 9am-6pm Sat, 11am-5pm Sun

2, 6, 9, 14, 21, 31, M Embarcadero, B Embarcadero

Cable car passing the Ferry Building

Don't Miss

Hog Island Oyster Company

Decadence with a conscience: sustainably farmed, local Tomales Bay oysters are served raw and cooked with Sonoma bubbly at **Hog Island** (☎415-391-7117; www.hogislandoysters.com; 4 oysters $13; ⏱11am-9pm). Oysters are half-price and pints $4 from 5pm to 7pm Monday to Thursday.

Boulette's Larder & Boulibar

Dinner theater doesn't get better than brunch at **Boulette's** (☎415-399-1155; www.bouletteslarder. com; mains $18-24; ⏱Larder 8am-10:30am & 11:30am-3pm Tue-Sat, 10am-2:30pm Sun, Boulibar 11:30am-9:30pm Tue-Fri, 11am-8pm Sat) communal table, in a working kitchen amid a swirl of chefs and with views of the Bay Bridge. At the adjoining Boulibar, enjoy beautifully blistered wood-fired pizzas with foodie people-watching.

Slanted Door

Taste the California dream at **Slanted Door** (☎415-861-8032; www.slanteddoor.com; mains $18-42; ⏱11am-4:30pm & 5:30-10pm Mon-Sat, 11:30am-4:30pm & 5:30-10pm Sun), where James Beard Award–winning chef-owner Charles Phan serves California-fresh, Vietnamese-inspired dishes with bay views. Book ahead, or picnic on takeout *banh mi* (sandwiches).

Mijita

Sustainable fish tacos reign supreme and *agua fresca* (fruit punch) is made with fresh juice at James Beard Award–winning chef-owner Traci Des Jardins' casual **Mijita** (☎415-399-0814; www. mijitasf.com; dishes $4-10; ⏱10am-7pm Mon-Thu, to 8pm Fri, 9am-8pm Sat, 9am-3pm Sun; 🍴🚼), paying tribute to her Mexican grandmother's cooking.

☑ Top Tips

▶ Among the locavore gourmet stalls lining the grand arrivals hall, don't miss dessert at Recchiuti Chocolates (p94).

▶ For bayside picnics, find benches flanking the bronze statue of Gandhi by the ferry docks, or head to Pier 14 for perches with bay views.

▶ Across the Embarcadero from the Ferry Building in Justin Hermann Plaza, lunchtime picnickers mingle with wild parrots, protestors, skaters and craftspeople.

✕ Take a Break

During the Tuesday, Thursday and Saturday **farmers markets** (Map p80, H2; ☎415-291-3276; www.cuesa.org; Market St & the Embarcadero; ⏱10am-2pm Tue & Thu, 8am-2pm Sat; Ⓜ Embarcadero), hit gourmet food stalls flanking the Ferry Building's southwestern corner.

Top Sights
Cable Cars

Roller-coaster rides can't compare to the death-defying thrills of riding a 15,000lb cable car down San Francisco hills, careening toward oncoming traffic. But Andrew Hallidie's 1873 contraptions have held up miraculously well on these giddy slopes, and groaning brakes and clanging brass bells add to the carnival-ride thrills. Powell-Mason cars are quickest to reach Fisherman's Wharf; Powell-Hyde cars are more scenic; and the original east–west California St line is the least crowded.

 Map p80, D2

cnr Powell & Market Sts

🚋 Powell-Mason, Mason-Hyde, Ⓜ Powell, Ⓑ Powell

Cable car on the Powell-Hyde line

Don't Miss

Powell-Hyde Cable Car

The journey is the destination on this hilly line, with the Golden Gate Bridge popping in and out of view. Hop off the cable car atop zig-zagging Lombard St to see pine-framed Golden Gate Bridge panoramas at George Sterling Park.

Powell-Mason Cable Car

Powell-Mason's ascent up Nob Hill feels like the world's longest roller-coaster climb. Leap off before the Fisherman's Wharf terminus to find your fortune (cookie) in Chinatown, explore North Beach's pizza possibilities or glimpse Diego Rivera murals at San Francisco Art Institute. (p42)

California Street Cable Car

History buffs and crowd-shy travelers prefer the California St line, in operation since 1878. This divine ride heads west through Chinatown, and climbs Nob Hill to Grace Cathedral (p71). The Van Ness terminus is a few blocks northeast of Japantown.

Powell Street Cable Car Turnaround

At Powell and Market Sts, operators slooowly turn Powell-Hyde and Powell-Mason cable cars around on a revolving wooden platform. Tourists line up here to secure a seat, with street performers and doomsday preachers for entertainment. Locals hop on further uphill.

☑ Top Tips

▶ Cable car lines operate 6am to 1am daily, with scheduled departures every three to 12 minutes; for schedules, see http://transit.511.org.

▶ If you're planning to stop en route, get a Muni Passport (per day $17). One-way tickets cost $7, with no on-and-off privileges.

▶ This 19th-century transport vehicle isn't childproof – you won't find car seats or seat belts. Kids love open-air seating, but it's safer to hold small children inside the car.

▶ Cable cars are not accessible for people with disabilities.

▶ Cable cars make rolling stops. To board on hills, act fast: leap onto the baseboard and grab the closest hand-strap.

✗ Take a Break

Hop off for Tonga Room (p71) Scorpion Bowls and indoor monsoons.

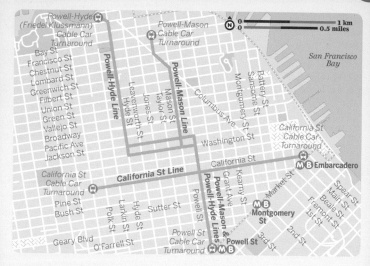

Powell-Hyde (Friedel Klussmann) Cable Car Turnaround

The Powell-Hyde turnaround at Fisherman's Wharf is named after the gardener who rallied her ladies' garden club in 1947 against the mayor's scheme to replace Powell cable cars with buses. In a public vote, the mayor lost to 'The Cable Car Lady' by a landslide. Upon her death in 1986, cable cars citywide were draped in black.

Understand
The Cable Car's Timeless Technology

Legend has it that the idea for cable cars came to Andrew Hallidie in 1869, after he watched a horse carriage struggle up Jackson St, slip on wet cobblestones, and crash downhill. Such accidents were considered inevitable on steep San Francisco hills, but Hallidie knew better. His father was the Scottish inventor of wire cable, used to haul ore out of Gold Rush mines. If hemp-and-metal cable could carry rock through Sierras snowstorms, surely it could transport San Franciscans through fog.

By the 1890s, 53 miles of cable car tracks crisscrossed San Francisco. Hallidie remained a lifelong inventor, earning 300 patents, and became a pioneering member of the California Academy of Sciences.

This vintage Victorian transport does have drawbacks. Cable cars can't move in reverse, and require burly gripmen – and one buff gripwoman – to hand-operate brakes to keep them from careening downhill. San Francisco receives many applicants for this job, but 80% fail the strenuous tests of upper-body strength and hand-eye coordination.

Yet Hallidie's cables seldom fray, and have rarely broken in more than a century of near-continuous operation. The key to the cable car's amazing safety record is the cable gripwheel, with clips that click into place and release gradually to prevent cable slips. This Victorian technology remains the killer app to conquer San Francisco's highest hills.

A B C D

0 _____ 400 m
0 _____ 0.2 miles

McAllister St
Elm St
Polk St
Larkin St
Ellis St
Leavenworth St
Geary St
O'Farrell St
28
Grove St
Van Ness Ave
Dr Carlton B Goodlett Pl
Hyde St
Turk St
Jones St
Taylor St
Mason St
Golden Gate Ave
Eddy St
Hayes St
Larkin St
McAllister St
Civic Center Plaza
Bank of America
Cable Cars
Fell St
San Francisco Main Library
United Nations Plaza
Powell St Cable Car Turnaround
Powell St
Market St
Civic Center
Stevenson St
Jessie St
Jessie St
34
Mission St
10th St
Grace St
9th St
8th St
7th St
Minna St
6th St
Mary St
5th St
Natoma St
Howard St
11th St
Dore Al
Tehama St
Langton St
Moss St
Russ St
Harriet St
Tehama St
Clementina St
SOUTH OF MARKET (SOMA)
25
29
21
Folsom St
22
Shipley St
Clara St
30
17
33
31
40
Victoria Manalo Draves Park
23
16
Harrison St
James Lick Skwy
Autoreturn
27
Morris St
Bryant St
32
Gilbert St
Harriet St
Brannan St
7th St
6th St
5th St
Bluxome St
26
Townsend St

For reviews see

E

F

CHINATOWN

G

Pacific Ave

12

Columbus Ave

Jackson St

Washington St

9

UNION SQUARE

California St

Transamerica Pyramid & Redwood Park

5

H

Walton Park

Maritime Plaza

35

Whaleship Plaza

Powell St

Pine St

Stockton St

Grant Ave

Sutter St

Kearny St

Bush St

Sacramento St

Montgomery St

Sansome St

Battery St

Embarcadero Center

The Embarcadero

1

Union Square

Post St

24

41

7

Wells Fargo History Museum

Front St

Justin Herman Plaza

Maiden La

37

13

19

American Automobile Association

Davis St

FINANCIAL DISTRICT (FIDI)

Ferry Building

2

10

49 Geary

36

6

42

Market St

California St Embarcadero

California St Cable Car Turnaround

38

14

Yerba Buena La

18

15

Montgomery St

Stevenson St

Audiffred Building

39

Pier 2

1

Contemporary Jewish Museum

4

California Historical Society Museum

Mission St

11

3

3

Museum of the African Diaspora

SFMOMA

Minna St

Children's Creativity Museum

2

8

New Montgomery St

Howard St

1st St

Fremont St

Beale St

Main St

Spear St

Steuart St

The Embarcadero

Folsom St

Folsom St

4th St

Bonifacio St

3rd St

Rizal St

Hawthorne St

2nd St

Folsom St

Harrison St

Pier 22½

4

James Lick Skwy

Pier 24

Bay Bridge

Pier 26

Bryant St

Zoe St

Ritch St

Taber Pl

South Park

Stanford St

2nd St

Delancey St

Embarcadero South St

Pier 28

Pier 30

Pier 32

San Francisco Bay

5

3rd St

Brannan St

Pier 34

Pier 36

Sights

Contemporary Jewish Museum

MUSEUM

1 ⊙ Map p80, E3

That upended brushed-steel box miraculously balancing on one corner isn't a sculpture, but the entry to the Contemporary Jewish Museum – and inside this building, any preconceived ideas about religion and art are also upended. Exhibits are compelling, provocative explorations of Jewish culture and ideals featuring artists as diverse as Andy Warhol and Amy

Winehouse, Gertrude Stein and Harry Houdini. The affectionately nicknamed 'Jewseum' invites theological and artistic debate over respectable pastrami, served on-site from 11am to 2pm by SF's Wise Sons Jewish Deli. (☎415-344-8800; www.thecjm.org; 736 Mission St; adult/child $12/free, after 5pm Thu $5, 1st Tue of month free; ⊙11am-5pm Mon-Tue & Fri-Sun, to 8pm Thu; ♿; ☐14, 30, 45, **M**Montgomery, **B**Montgomery)

Children's Creativity Museum

MUSEUM

2 ⊙ Map p80, E3

No velvet ropes or hands-off signs here: kids rule, with high-tech displays double-daring them to make music videos, claymation movies and soundtracks. Jump into live-action video games and sign up for workshops with Bay Area superstar animators, techno whizzes and robot builders. For low-tech fun, take a spin on the vintage-1906 **Loof Carousel** outside, operating 10am to 5pm daily; one $4 ticket covers two rides (you get $1 off with museum admission). (☎415-820-3320; http://creativity.org; 221 4th St; admission $12; ⊙10am-4pm Tue-Sun; ♿; ☐14, **M**Powell, **B**Powell)

Museum of the African Diaspora

MUSEUM

3 ⊙ Map p80, E3

MoAD assembles an international cast of characters to tell the epic story of diaspora, including a moving video of slave narratives told by Maya Angelou.

Standouts among quarterly changing exhibits have included contemporary Afro-Cuban art, post-colonial Nigerian fashion statements, and radical '60s graphics by African American printmaker and social activist Elizabeth Catlett. Public dialogues put art in context, with lively discussions on such current topics as African American archetypes in Hollywood, African masculinity, and the Black Lives Matter movement. (MoAD; ☎415-358-7200; www.moadsf.org; 685 Mission St; adult/student/child $10/5/free; ☉11am-6pm Wed-Sat, noon-5pm Sun; 🅿🚹; 🚌14, 30, 45, Ⓜ Montgomery, Ⓑ Montgomery)

California Historical Society Museum
MUSEUM

4 ◎ Map p80, E3

Enter a Golden State of enlightenment at this Californiana treasure trove, featuring themed exhibitions drawn from the museum's million-plus California photographs, paintings and ephemera. Recent exhibits have unearthed 19th-century photographs of pioneers gleefully climbing trees in Yosemite, scrapped designs for a futuristic Ferry Building, and the epic life story of fiercely independent Californian businesswoman Juana Briones, whose 1837 farmstead is now SF's North Beach neighborhood. (☎415-357-1848; www.californiahistoricalsociety.org; 678 Mission St; adult/child $5/free; ☉gallery & store 11am-8pm Tue, to 5pm Wed-Sun, library noon-5pm Wed-Fri; 🚹; Ⓜ Montgomery, Ⓑ Montgomery)

BUYENLARGE / GETTY IMAGES ©

Transamerica Pyramid

Transamerica Pyramid & Redwood Park
NOTABLE BUILDING

5 ◎ Map p80, G1

The defining feature of San Francisco's skyline is this 1972 pyramid, built atop the wreck of a whaling ship abandoned in the Gold Rush. A half-acre redwood grove sprouted out front, on the site of Mark Twain's favorite saloon and the office where Sun Yat-sen drafted his Proclamation of the Republic of China. Although these redwoods have shallow roots, their intertwined root network allows them to reach dizzying heights. Mark Twain couldn't have scripted a more perfect metaphor for San Francisco. (www.thepyramidcenter.com; 600 Montgomery St; ☉9am-6pm Mon-Fri; Ⓜ Embarcadero, Ⓑ Embarcadero)

49 Geary
ART GALLERY

6 Map p80, E2

Pity the collectors silently nibbling endive in austere Chelsea galleries – at 49 Geary, openings mean unexpected art, goldfish-shaped crackers and outspoken crowds. Four floors of galleries feature standout international and local works, from 19th to 21st century photography at Fraenkel Gallery to Andy Goldsworthy installation art at Haines Gallery and sculptor Seth Koen's minimalist pieces at Gregory Lind. For quieter contemplation, visit weekdays. (www.sfada.com; 49 Geary St; admission free; ⏰10:30am-5:30pm

Local Life
SFMOMA Expansion

From the start in 1935, **San Francisco Museum of Modern Art** (Map p80, E3; SFMOMA; ☎415-357-4000; www.sfmoma.org; 151 3rd St; ☐5, 6, 7, 14, 19, 21, 31, 38, Ⓜ Montgomery, Ⓑ Montgomery) defied convention and invested early in photography, installations, video and other thenexperimental media. Once the collection moved into architect Mario Botta's light-filled brick box in 1995, SFMOMA showed its backside to New York and leaned full-tilt toward the western horizon, pushing the art world to new media, new artists and new ideas. Currently undergoing a half-billion-dollar, 235,000-sq-ft expansion to house expanded collections, the museum is reopening in summer 2016.

Tue-Fri, 11am-5pm Sat; ☐5, 6, 7, 9, 21, 31, 38, Ⓜ Powell, Ⓑ Powell)

Wells Fargo History Museum
MUSEUM

7 Map p80, F2

Gold miners needed somewhere to stash and send cash, so Wells Fargo opened in this location in 1852. Today this storefront museum covers Gold Rush–era innovations, including the Pony Express, transcontinental telegrams and statewide stagecoaches. Wells Fargo was the world's largest stagecoach operator circa 1866, and you can climb aboard a preserved stagecoach to hear pioneer-trail stories while kids ride a free mechanical pony. Notwithstanding blatant PR for Wells Fargo, the exhibits are well-researched, fascinating and free. (☎415-396-2619; www.wellsfargohistory. com/museums; 420 Montgomery St; admission free; ⏰9am-5pm Mon-Fri; ♿; Ⓜ Montgomery, Ⓑ Montgomery)

Eating

Benu
CALIFORNIAN, FUSION **$$$**

8 Map p80, F3

SF has set fusion cuisine standards for 150 years, but chef-owner Corey Lee remixes California ingredients and Pacific Rim inspiration with a superstar DJ's finesse. Dungeness crab and truffle custard bring such outsize flavor to Lee's faux-shark's-fin soup, you'll swear there's Jaws in there. The prix-fixe menu is pricey (plus 20% service), but don't miss star-sommelier Yoon Ha's ingenious pairings ($160). (📞415-685-4860; www.benusf.com; 22 Hawthorne St; tasting menu $228; ⏱seatings 5:30-8:30pm Tue-Sat; 🚌10, 12, 14, 30, 45)

Kusakabe

SUSHI, JAPANESE **$$$**

9 Map p80, G1

Trust chef Mitsunori Kusakabe's *omakase* (tasting menu). Soy sauce isn't provided, nor missed. Sit at the counter while chef adds an herbal hint to fatty tuna with the *inside* of a shiso leaf. After you devour the menu – mostly with your hands, 'to release flavors' – you can special-order Hokkaido sea urchin, which chef perfumes with the *outside* of the shiso leaf. Brilliant. (📞415-757-0155; http://kusakabe-sf.com; 584 Washington St; prix-fixe $95; ⏱5-10pm, last seating 8:30pm; 🚌8, 10, 12, 41)

Tout Sweet

BAKERY **$**

10 Map p80, E2

Sour cherry and bourbon, or peanut butter and jelly? Choosing your new favorite French macaron flavor isn't easy at Tout Sweet, where *Top Desserts* champion Yigit Pura keeps outdoing his own inventions – he's like the lovechild of Julia Child and Steve Jobs. Chef Pura's sweet retreat on the 3rd floor of Macy's also offers unbeatable views of Union Square, excellent teas and free wi-fi. (📞415-385-1679; www.tout sweetsf.com; Geary & Stockton Sts, Macy's, 3rd fl; baked goods $2-8; ⏱10am-8pm Mon-Wed, to 9pm Thu-Sat, 11am-7pm Sun; 🛜♿; 🚌2, 38, 🚋Powell-Mason, Powell-Hyde, Ⓑ Powell St)

Boulevard

CALIFORNIAN **$$$**

11 Map p80, H3

The 1889 belle epoque Audiffred Building was once the Coast Seamen's Union, but for the last 20-plus years James Beard Award–winning chef Nancy Oakes has made culinary history with Boulevard. Reliably tasty, effortlessly elegant menu signatures include juicy oven-roasted Kurobuta pork chops, crisp California quail and dumplings, and grilled Pacific salmon

---

Local Life
San Francisco Murals at Rincon Annex Post Office

Only in San Francisco could a post office be so controversial. Art deco **Rincon Annex Post Office** (Map p80, H3; 101 Spear St; admission free; 🚌2, 6, 7, 14, 21, 31, ⓂEmbarcadero, ⒷEmbarcadero) is lined with vibrant Works Project Administration murals of San Francisco history, begun by Russian-born painter Anton Refregier in 1941 – but WWII and political squabbles over differing versions of San Francisco history caused delays. After 92 changes to satisfy censors, Refregier finally concluded the mural cycle in 1948 with *War & Peace,* pointedly contrasting scenes of Nazi book-burning and postwar promises of 'freedom from fear/want/of worship/speech.' Initially denounced as communist by McCarthyists, Refregier's masterpiece is now protected as a national landmark.

with wild morel mushrooms – plus sticky toffee pudding with black-pepper ice cream. (☎415-543-6084; www.boulevardrestaurant.com; 1 Mission St; mains lunch $18-31, dinner $29-48; ⏱11:30am-2:15pm & 5:30-10pm Mon-Thu, to 10:30pm Fri & Sat, 5:30-10pm Sun; Ⓜ Embarcadero, Ⓑ Embarcadero)

Trestle CALIFORNIAN $$

 12 Map p80, G1

Whether your fortunes are up or down in SF, you're in luck here: $35 brings three courses of tasty rustic comfort food. You get two options per course – typically soup or salad, meat or seafood, fruity or chocolatey dessert – so you and your date can taste the entire menu. Get the bonus handmade pasta course ($10). Seating is tight but friendly. (☎415-772-0922; http://trestlesf.com; 531 Jackson St; 3-course meal $35; ⏱5:30-10:30pm Mon-Thu, to 11pm Fri & Sat, to 10pm Sun; 🚌8, 10, 12, 30, 45)

Sushirrito JAPANESE, FUSION $

 13 Map p80, F2

Ever get a sushi craving, but you're hungry enough for a burrito? Join the crowd at Sushirrito, where fresh Latin and Asian ingredients are rolled in rice and nori, then conveniently wrapped in foil. Pan-Pacific Rim flavors shine in Geisha's Kiss, with line-caught yellowfin tuna and piquillo peppers, and the vegetarian Buddha Belly, with spicy Japanese eggplant, kale and avocado. (☎415-544-9868; www.sushirrito.com; 226 Kearny St; dishes $9-13; ⏱11am-4pm Mon-

Thu, to 7pm Fri, noon-4pm Sat; 🥢; 🚌30, 45, Ⓑ Montgomery, Ⓜ Montgomery)

Tropisueño MEXICAN $$

 14 Map p80, E3

Last time you enjoyed casual Mexican dining this much, there were probably balmy ocean breezes and hammocks involved. Instead, you're steps away from SoMa's museums, savoring *al pastor* (marinated pork) burritos with mesquite salsa and grilled pineapple, sipping margaritas with chili-salted rims. The rustic-organic decor is definitely downtown, but prices are down to earth. (☎415-243-0299; www.tropisueno.com; 75 Yerba Buena Lane; mains lunch $7-12, dinner $14-18; ⏱11am-10:30pm; 🚌8, 14, 30, 45, Ⓜ Powell, Ⓑ Powell)

Sentinel SANDWICHES $

 15 Map p80, F3

Rebel SF chef Dennis Leary is out to revolutionize lunchtime takeout with top-notch seasonal ingredients. Tuna salad gets radical with chipotle mayo and artichokes, and corned beef crosses borders with Swiss cheese and housemade Russian dressing. Check the website for daily menus and call in your order, or else expect a 10-minute wait – sandwiches are made to order. Enjoy in the Crocker Galleria rooftop garden. (☎415-284-9960; www.thesentinelsf.com; 37 New Montgomery St; sandwiches $9-10.50; ⏱7:30am-2:30pm Mon-Fri; 🚌12, 14, Ⓜ Montgomery, Ⓑ Montgomery)

SoMa StrEat Food Park

FOOD TRUCKS $

16 Map p80, A4

Your posse is hungry, but one of you is vegan, another wants burritos and beer, and another only likes burritos made with Korean barbecue beef. So what do you do? First: recognize that you and your friends belong in San Francisco. Second: head to this SoMa parking lot where the food trucks can satisfy your every whim. The area gets sketchy – mind your wallet. (http://somastreatfoodpark.com; 428 11th St; dishes $5-12; ⏰11am-3pm & 5-9pm Mon-Fri, 11am-10pm Sat, to 5pm Sun; ☐9, 27, 47)

Bar Agricole

Drinking

Bar Agricole

BAR

17 🚇 Map p80, A4

Drink your way to a history degree with well-researched cocktails: Bellamy Scotch Sour with house bitters and egg whites passes the test, but El Presidente with white rum, farmhouse curaçao and California pomegranate grenadine takes top honors. This overachiever racks up James Beard Award nods for its spirits and eco-savvy design, and pairs decadent drink with local oysters and excellent California cheeses. (📞415-355-9400; www.baragricole.com; 355 11th St; ⏰6-10pm Sun-Thu, 5:30-11pm Fri & Sat; ☐9, 12, 27, 47)

Local Edition

BAR

18 🚇 Map p80, E2

Get the scoop on the SF cocktail scene at this new speakeasy in the basement of the historic Hearst newspaper building. Lighting is so dim you might bump into typewriters, but all is forgiven when you get The Pulitzer – a scotch-sherry cocktail that goes straight to your head. (📞415-795-1375; www.localeditionsf.com; 691 Market St; ⏰5pm-2am Mon-Fri, from 7pm Sat; ⓂMontgomery, ⒷMontgomery)

Rickhouse

BAR

19 🚇 Map p80, F2

Like a shotgun shack plunked downtown, Rickhouse is lined floor-to-ceiling with repurposed whiskey casks imported from Kentucky and back-bar shelving from an Ozark Mountains nunnery that once secretly brewed hooch. The emphasis is (naturally) on whiskey, specifically hard-to-find bourbons – but the cocktails are sublime. Round up a posse to help finish that garage-sale punchbowl of Pisco Punch. (☎415-398-2827; www.rick housebar.com; 246 Kearny St; ☉5pm-2am Mon, 3pm-2am Tue-Fri, 6pm-2am Sat; ☐8, 30, 45, Ⓜ Montgomery, Ⓑ Montgomery)

BeatBox

GAY & LESBIAN

20 Map p80, A4

The warehouse dance club at the end of the rainbow, where the wooden floors, beers and men can take a pounding. Most nights are mixed-gender queer – check out who's smoking/hot on the sidewalk before you enter. Women rule at UHaul, Red Hots Burlesque bring circus-freak fabulousness, men totally get Served and Bearracuda is America's biggest, barest bear party. (☎415-500-2675; http://beatboxsf.com; 314 11th St; cover free-$30; ☉10pm-2am; ☐9, 12, 27, 47)

Cat Club

CLUB

21 Map p80, B4

You never really know your friends till you've seen them belt out A-ha's 'Take on Me' at Class of '84, Cat Club's Thursday-night retro dance party, where the euphoric bi/straight/gay/undefinable scene is like some sweaty, surreal John Hughes movie. Tuesdays it's free karaoke, Wednesdays Bondage-a-Go-Go, Fridays Goth

and Saturdays '80s to '90s power pop – RSVP online for $3 off entry. (www. sfcatclub.com; 1190 Folsom St; cover free-$10 after 10pm; ☉9pm-3am Tue-Sat; ☐12, 19, 27, 47, Ⓜ Civic Center, Ⓑ Civic Center)

Bloodhound

BAR

22 Map p80, B4

The murder of crows painted on the ceiling is an omen: nights at Bloodhound often assume mythic proportions. Vikings would feel at home amid these antler chandeliers, while bootleggers would appreciate barnwood walls and top-shelf hooch served in Mason jars. Shoot pool or chill on leather couches until your jam comes on the jukebox. (☎415-863-2840; www.bloodhoundsf.com; 1145 Folsom St; ☉4pm-2am; ☐12, 14, 19, 27, 47)

Eagle Tavern

GAY, BAR

23 Map p80, A4

Sunday afternoons, all roads in the gay underground lead to the Eagle, and the crowd gets hammered on all-you-can-drink beer ($10) from 3pm to 6pm. Wear leather – or flirt shamelessly – and blend right in; arrive before 3pm to beat long lines. Thursdays bring mixed crowds for rockin' bands; Fridays and Saturdays range from bondage to drag. Check online. (www.sf-eagle.com; 398 12th St; cover $5-10; ☉2pm-2am Mon-Fri, from noon Sat & Sun; ☐9, 12, 27, 47)

Understand
Bay Bridge

Artist Leo Villareal's installation of twinkling lights along the western span will make you swear the Bay Bridge (www.baybridgeinfo.org) is winking at you. In 2013 Villareal strung 25,000 lights along the Bay Bridge's vertical suspension cables, transforming the 1.8-mile western span into the world's largest and most psychedelic LED display.

The Bay Bridge Lights blink in never-repeating patterns – one second the bridge looks like bubbly champagne, then a lava-lamp forest, then Vegas-style swaying fountains. You could stare at it for hours...hopefully not while driving. The installation was meant to be temporary, but thanks to local donors, it will be permanently installed in 2016.

The razzle-dazzle western span competes with the new eastern span, which opened to cars in September 2013. A sore subject for San Francisco taxpayers, this span – damaged in the 1989 Loma Prieta earthquake – took 12 years to build and cost taxpayers $6.4 billion.

Bay Bridge boosters and detractors alike agree: the bridge was the idea of a certifiable madman. Joshua Norton arrived in San Francisco from South Africa in 1849, made and lost a fortune, and disappeared – then returned a decade later, proclaiming himself 'Emperor of the United States and Protector of Mexico.' San Francisco newspapers published Emperor Norton's decrees fining users of the term 'Frisco' $25 (payable to His Highness) and ordering construction in 1872 of a trans-bay bridge. Petitions have circulated since 2004 to officially name the span the Emperor Norton Bay Bridge – though no one can agree whether it's a compliment or an insult.

Irish Bank
PUB

 24 Map p80, F2

Perfectly pulled pints and thick-cut fries with malt vinegar, plus juicy burgers, brats and anything else you could possibly want with lashings of mustard are staples at this cozy Irish pub. There are tables beneath a big awning in the alley out front, ideal for smokers – even on a rainy night. (☑415-788-7152; www.theirishbank.com; 10 Mark Lane; ☉11:30am-2am; ☐2, 3, 30, 45, ⓜMontgomery, ⓑMontgomery)

Sightglass Coffee
CAFÉ

 25 Map p80, B3

Follow the aroma of cult coffee into this sunny SoMa warehouse, where family-grown, high-end bourbon-shrub coffee is roasted daily. Aficionados sip signature Owl's Howl Espresso around the downstairs bar – but for the ultimate pick-me-up, head to the mezzanine Affogato Bar for a scoop of creamy gelato in your coffee. Caffeinated socializing is encouraged; no

wi-fi or outlets. (☎415–861–1313; www.
sightglasscoffee.com; 270 7th St; ☺7am-7pm;
🚌12, 14, 19, Ⓜ Civic Center, Ⓑ Civic Center)

Bluxome Street Winery   WINE BAR

26 Map p80, D5

Rolling vineyards seem overrated
once you've visited SoMA's finest
back-alley winery. Grab a barrel-top
stool and watch winemakers at work
in the adjoining warehouse while you
sip Syrah rosé. Food trucks park out

front; trust your pourer to provide
the perfect Russian River Pinot Noir
for that pork-belly taco. Call ahead,
or you might accidentally crash a
start-up launch. (☎415-543-5353; www.
bluxomewinery.com; 53 Bluxome St; ☺noon-
7pm Tue-Sun; Ⓜ N, T)

EndUp   GAY, CLUB

27 Map p80, C4

Forget the Golden Gate Bridge: once
you EndUp watching the sunrise over
the 101 freeway ramp, you've officially
arrived in SF. Dance sessions are
marathons fueled by EndUp's 24-hour
license, so Saturday nights have a way
of turning into Monday mornings.
Straight people sometimes EndUp
here – but gay Sunday tea dances are
legendary, in full force since 1973.
(☎415-646-0999; www.theendup.com; 401
6th St; cover $5-20; ☺9:30pm-8am Fri,
10pm-6am Sat, 6am-noon & 2-10pm Sun;
🚌12, 19, 27, 47)

Entertainment

American Conservatory Theater   THEATER

28 Map p80, D1

Breakthrough shows launch at this
turn-of-the-century landmark, which
has hosted ACT's landmark produc-
tions of Tony Kushner's *Angels in
America* and Robert Wilson's *Black
Rider*, with William S Burroughs'
libretto and music by Tom Waits.
Major playwrights like Tom Stoppard,

David Mamet and Sam Shepard premiere work here, while experimental works are staged at ACT's new **Strand Theater** (1127 Market St). (ACT; ☎415-749-2228; www.act-sf.org; 415 Geary St; ⏰box office noon-6pm Mon, to curtain Tue-Sun; ☒8, 30, 38, 45, ☒Powell-Mason, Powell-Hyde, ☒Powell, ☒Powell)

Oasis

CABARET, LGBT

29 ⭐ Map p80, A4

Forget what you've learned about drag from TV – at this dedicated dragstravaganza venue, SF drag is so fearless, freaky-deaky and funny you'll laugh until it stops hurting. SF drag icons Heklina and D'Arcy Drollinger host variety acts, put on original shows like '70s-'ploitation *Sh*t & Champagne,* and perform drag versions of *Sex in the City* (makes 393% more sense in drag). (☎415-795-3180; www.sfoasis.com; 298 11th St; tickets $10-30; ☒9, 12, 14, 47, ☒Van Ness)

Slim's

LIVE MUSIC

30 ⭐ Map p80, A4

Guaranteed good times by Gogol Bordello, Stiff Little Fingers, Veruca Salt and Killer Queen (an all-female Queen tribute band) fit the bill at this midsized club, owned by R&B star Boz Scaggs. Shows are all-ages, though shorties may have a hard time seeing once the floor starts bouncing. Reserve dinner for an additional $25 and score seats on the small balcony. (☎415-255-0333; www.slimspresents.com; 333 11th St; tickets $12-30; ⏰box office

Union Square

10:30am-6pm Mon-Fri & on show nights; ☒9, 12, 27, 47)

Stud

GAY, CLUB

31 ⭐ Map p80, A4

The Stud has rocked the gay scene since 1966. Anything goes at Meow Mix Tuesday drag variety shows; Thursdays bring raunchy comedy and karaoke. But Friday's the thing, when the freaky 'Some-thing' party brings bizarre midnight art-drag, pool-table crafts and dance-ready beats. Saturdays, various DJs spin – kick-ass GoBang is among the best. Check the online calendar. (www.studsf.com; 399 9th St; cover $5-8; ⏰noon-2am Tue, 5pm-3am Thu-Sat, 5pm-midnight Sun; ☒12, 19, 27, 47)

Hotel Utah Saloon

LIVE MUSIC

32 Map p80, D5

This Victorian saloon ruled SF's '70s underground scene, when upstarts Whoopi Goldberg and Robin Williams took the stage – and fresh talents regularly surface here on Monday Night Open Mics, indie-label debuts and twangy weekend showcases. Back in the '50s, the bartender graciously served Beats and drifters, but snipped off businessmen's ties; now you can wear whatever, but there's a $20 credit-card minimum. (☎415-546-6300; www.hotelutah.com; 500 4th St; cover free-$10; ☉11:30am-2am; 🚌30, 47, Ⓜ️N, T)

DNA Lounge

CLUB

33 ⭐ Map p80, A4

SF's reigning mega-club hosts bands, literary slams and big-name DJs, with two floors of late-night dance action just seedy enough to be interesting. Saturdays bring Bootie, the original mash-up party (now franchised worldwide); Fridays Mortified writers read from their teenage diaries; Goth/industrial bands play Sunday's 18-and-over Death Guild; Mondays mean Hubba Hubba burlesque revues. Check calendar; early arrivals may hear crickets. (☎415-626-1409; www.dnalounge.com; 375 11th St; cover $9-35; ☉9pm-5am; 🚌9, 12, 27, 47)

Mezzanine

LIVE MUSIC

34 ⭐ Map p80, D3

Big nights come with bragging rights at the Mezzanine, with one of the city's best sound systems and crowds hyped for breakthrough shows by hip-hop greats like Wyclef Jean and Quest Love, EDM powerhouses like Knife Party, mash-up artists like Lido (think Bill Withers meets Disclosure), plus Throwback Thursdays featuring power-pop legends like Howard Jones. No in/out privileges. (☎415-625-8880; www.mezzaninesf.com; 444 Jessie St; cover $10-40; Ⓜ️Powell, Ⓑ Powell)

◯ Local Life

San Francisco Giants

Hometown crowds go wild April to October for the San Francisco Giants at **AT&T Park** (Map p80, F5; AT&T Park; ☎415-972-2000, tour 415-972-2400; http://sanfrancisco.giants.mlb.com; tickets $14-280, tour adult/child $22/12; ☉tour 10:30am & 2:30pm; 👶; Ⓜ️N, T). The city's National League baseball team won the 2010, 2012 and 2014 World Series with superstitious practices that endear them to SF: players sport bushy beards and pitchers may be wearing women's underwear. Behind-the-scenes tours cover the clubhouse, dugout, field and solar-powered scoreboard. When games sell out, you might score tickets through the Double Play Ticket Window (see website) – or glimpse free views of right field along the Waterfront Promenade.

Punch Line
COMEDY

35 ⭐ Map p80, G1

Known for launching big talent – including Robin Williams, Chris Rock, Ellen DeGeneres and David Cross – this historic stand-up venue is small enough for you to hear sighs of relief backstage when jokes kill, and teeth grind when they bomb. Strong drinks loosen up the crowd, but be warned: you might not be laughing tomorrow. (📞415-397-7573; www.punchlinecomedyclub. com; 444 Battery St; cover $15-25, plus 2-drink minimum; ⏰shows 8pm Tue-Thu & Sun, 8pm & 10pm Fri, 7:30pm & 9:30pm Sat; Ⓜ Embarcadero, Ⓑ Embarcadero)

Shopping

Harputs
CLOTHING, ACCESSORIES

36 🔒 Map p80, E2

Superheroes have to squeeze into phone booths and tights to make their transformations, but you can just duck into Harputs to summon your SF alter ego with a ninja romper, fog-stopping swacket (sweater jacket) or peace-making dress (straps form a peace sign on your shoulders). Designs involve clever wraps and flattering folds that show off your shape, smarts and wit. (📞415-392-2222; www. harputs.com; 109 Geary St, 2nd fl; ⏰11am-7pm Mon-Sat; 🚌6, 7, 38, Ⓜ Montgomery, Ⓑ Montgomery)

 Local Life
Modern Dance at Yerba Buena

Modern dance pioneer Isadora Duncan hailed from San Francisco, and you can see SF's latest bold, modern moves at **Yerba Buena Center for the Arts** (Map p80, E3; YBCA; 📞415-978-2700; www.ybca.org; 700 Howard St; tickets free-$35; ⏰box office noon-6pm Sun & Tue-Wed, to 8pm Thu-Sat, galleries closed Mon-Tue; ♿; 🚌14, Ⓜ Powell, Ⓑ Powell). The main stage hosts regular seasons of notable SF modern dance companies: **Liss Fain Dance** (📞415-380-9433; www.lissfaindance.org), champions of muscular modern movement; **Alonzo King's Lines Ballet** (📞415-863-3040; www.linesballet.org), known for angular, architectural formations; **Smuin Ballet** (📞415-912-1899; www.smuinballet.org; ⏰box office phone line 1-5pm Tue-Fri), with relatable dance befitting its tagline, 'Ballet, but Entertaining.' **Dancers' Group** (www.dancersgroup.org) keeps a comprehensive performance calendar.

Britex Fabrics
FABRIC

37 🔒 Map p80, E2

Runway shows can't compete with Britex's fashion drama. First floor: designers bicker over dibs on caution-orange chiffon. Second floor: glam rockers dig through velvet goldmines. Third floor: Hollywood costumers make vampire movie magic with jet buttons and silk ribbon. Top floor:

fake fur flies and remnants roll as costumers prepare for Burning Man, Halloween and your average SF weekend. (📞415-392-2910; www.britexfabrics. com; 146 Geary St; ⏰10am-6pm Mon-Sat; 🚌38, 🚋Powell-Mason, Powell-Hyde, Ⓜ️Powell, Ⓑ Powell)

Recchiuti Chocolates FOOD & DRINK

38 🔒 Map p80, H2

No San Franciscan can resist Recchiuti: Pacific Heights parts with old money for its *fleur de sel* caramels; Noe Valley's foodie kids prefer S'more Bites to the campground variety; North Beach toasts to the red-wine-pairing chocolate box; and the Mission approves SF landmark chocolates designed by developmentally disabled artists from Creativity Explored (p118) – part of the proceeds benefit the nonprofit gallery. (📞415-834-9494; www.recchiuticonfections.

com; 1 Ferry Bldg; ⏰10am-7pm Mon-Fri, 8am-6pm Sat, 10am-5pm Sun; Ⓜ️Embarcadero, Ⓑ Embarcadero)

San Francisco Railway Museum Gift Shop
GIFTS

39 🔒 Map p80, H3

The next best thing to taking an SF cable car home with you is getting a scale model streetcar from this tiny free Municipal Railway museum showcasing SF public transit. Earn instant SF street cred with baseball caps and T-shirts emblazoned with Muni slogans, including everyone's favorite: 'Information gladly given, but safety requires avoiding unnecessary conversation.' (📞415-974-1948; www.streetcar. org/museum; 77 Steuart St; ⏰10am-6pm Tue-Sun; 🚌Embarcadero, Ⓑ Embarcadero)

Understand
SF Chain Stores

Young Levi Strauss brought fashion sense to the Gold Rush in 1850, making pants from tough French sailcloth from Nîmes ('de Nîmes,' or denim) to hold heavy nuggets. Levi's flagship store at 815 Market St stocks limited-edition releases of vintage models – 1950s prison-model denim sells out fast.

The Gap/Old Navy/Banana Republic retail juggernaut also started out in San Francisco as a single Gap store selling wardrobe basics. Yet these and other global mega-brands, including Uniqlo, H&M and Urban Outfitters, are largely confined downtown in Westfield Mall, around Union Square and along Powell St – they're kept out of neighborhoods by city zoning resolutions and snarky vandalism. Read one graffiti correction to a 'Peace. Love. Gap.' bus-shelter ad: 'It's Peace, Love & Understanding, you corporate tools.'

Madame S & Mr S Leather
CLOTHING, ACCESSORIES

 40 Map p80, B4

Only in San Francisco would you find an S&M superstore, with such musts as suspension stirrups, latex hoods and, for that special someone, a chrome-plated codpiece. If you've been a very bad puppy, there's an entire doghouse department catering to you here, and gluttons for punishment will find home-decor inspiration in Dungeon Furniture. (☎415-863-7764; www.mr-s-leather.com; 385 8th St; ☻11am-8pm; ☒12, 19, 27, 47)

Margaret O'Leary
CLOTHING, ACCESSORIES

41 Map p80, F2

Ignorance of the fog is no excuse in San Francisco, but should you confuse SF for LA (the horror!) and neglect to pack the obligatory sweater, Margaret O'Leary will sheathe you in knitwear, no questions asked. The SF designer's specialties are warm, whisper-light cardigans in Scottish cashmere, cotton and silk. (☎415-391-1010; www.margaretoleary.com; 1 Claude Lane; ☻10am-5pm Tue-Sat; ☒8, 30, 45, Ⓜ Montgomery, Ⓑ Montgomery)

T-We Tea
FOOD & DRINK

42 Map p80, F2

Start days the SF way with T-We tea to match your attitude: sprawl in

Hotel Utah Saloon (p92)

Dolores Park with Hipsters in Wonderland (green tea, jasmine, carrot chips), huddle like Sunset surfers over Foggy Morning Brekkie (four-tea blend with vanilla bean), or recover from SoMa clubs with Bad Bromance (nettle-ginger afterparty tisane). T-We blends teas in SF with sass and local flavor, nothing artificial. (www.t-wetea.com; Crocker Galleria, 50 Post St, Level 1; ☻10am-6pm Mon-Fri; Ⓑ Montgomery, Ⓜ Montgomery)

Explore

Hayes Valley & Civic Center

Don't be fooled by its grand formality – San Francisco's Civic Center is down-to-earth and cutting edge. City Hall helped launch gay rights and green schemes, and arts institutions nearby ensure San Francisco is never lost for inspiration. West of City Hall lies Hayes Valley, where jazz accompanies skateboarders, Victorian storefronts showcase upstart designers and creative crowds socialize in shipping containers.

The Sights in a Day

 Get a fresh start at **farm:table** (p105), then hop the historic F-line streetcar to the **Asian Art Museum** (p98). Here you'll cover the Silk Road in an hour, from Persian miniatures to Chinese snuff bottles. Across the plaza at **City Hall** (pictured left; p102), you can see where sit-ins, gay marriage and zero-waste mandates made US history.

Browse boutiques down Hayes St to sensational **Souvla** (p104) salads, followed by curbside **Blue Bottle Coffee** (p106). Hit the comics lounge at **Isotope** (p110), get fog-dewy skin at **Nancy Boy** (p109) and try SF history on for size at **Paloma** (p109).

Haul your booty to pirate-themed speakeasy **Smuggler's Cove** (p105) – but don't let that Dead Reckoning cocktail delay dinner at **Rich Table** (p103) or your grand entrance at **San Francisco Symphony** (p107), **San Francisco Opera** (p107) or **SFJAZZ** (p108). End your night in a compromising position at **Hemlock Tavern** (p109), and you've done SF proud.

 Top Sight

Asian Art Museum (p98)

Best of San Francisco

Live Music
San Francisco Symphony (p107)
San Francisco Opera (p107)
SFJAZZCenter (p108)
Great American Music Hall (p108)
Warfield (p109)

Drinks
Smuggler's Cove (p105)
Bourbon & Branch (p105)
Blue Bottle Coffee Company (p106)
Hôtel Biron (p106)
Hemlock Tavern (p109)
Rye (p106)

Getting There

Streetcar Historic F Market streetcars run along Market St; J, K, L, M and N metro lines run under Market St to Van Ness and Civic Center stations.

Bus Lines 2, 5, 6, 7, 21 and 31 run down Market to Civic Center toward Hayes Valley; lines 47 and 49 run along Van Ness.

Car Garage under Civic Center Plaza.

Top Sights
Asian Art Museum

Sightsee halfway across the globe in an hour, from romantic Persian miniatures to daring Chinese installation art – just don't go bumping into those priceless Ming vases. The museum's curators work diplomatic wonders here, bringing Taiwan, China and Tibet together, uniting Pakistan and India, and reconciling Japan, Korea and China under one Italianate roof. The distinguished collection of 18,000 unique treasures also does the city proud, reflecting San Francisco's 165-year history as North America's gateway to Asia.

Map p100

www.asianart.org

200 Larkin St

adult/student/child $15/10/ free, 1st Sun of month free

⊙10am-5pm Tue-Sun, to 9pm Thu

Ⓜ Civic Center, Ⓑ Civic Center

Asian Art Museum

Don't Miss

Permanent Collection

The Asian Art Museum's curatorial concept is to follow the evolution of Asian art from West to East toward San Francisco, along Buddhist pilgrimage trails and trade routes. Granted, the Chinese collection takes up two wings and South Asia only one – but that healthy cultural competition has encouraged donations of South Asian artifacts lately.

Start your tour on the 3rd floor with a treasure trove of Indian miniatures and jewels. Detour through dizzying Iranian geometric tiles and Javanese shadow puppets, and turn a corner to find Tibetan prayer wheels. Ahead is a 3000-year-old Chinese bronze rhinoceros wine vessel with a twinkle in its eye, plus Chinese jades and snuff bottles. Downstairs on the 2nd floor are calligraphy, Korean celadon bowls and an entire Japanese tea ceremony room.

Contemporary Shows

As you wander through 6000 years of Asian art, look for artworks by contemporary artists responding to pieces in the collection. Rotating ground-floor exhibits spotlight exceptional collections and groundbreaking artists. Artists Drawing Club events held upstairs in Samsung Hall invite visitors to collaborate in a contemporary artist's art-making process.

Architecture

Italian architect Gae Aulenti's clever repurposing of the old San Francisco Main Library building left intact the much-beloved granite bas-relief on the building's facade, travertine entry arches and the grand stone staircase. She added two new indoor courts for oversize installations, leaving plenty of room for debate and educational programs.

☑ Top Tips

▶ On Thursday nights (5pm to 9pm, February through September), the Asian gets hip with cross-cultural mash-up DJs and special guests – lately, Asian American slam poets, Korean quilters, and Olympian martial artists kicking with lethal force.

▶ Parents can pick up **Explorer Cards** for kids to find favorite animals and characters in the galleries.

▶ Check the schedule for live artists' demonstrations, free yoga classes and hands-on workshops for kids.

✖ Take a Break

On the museum's sunny terrace at **Café Asia** (Map p100, E4; www. asianart.org/visit/cafe-asia; 200 Larkin St; mains $5-14; ☉10am-4:30pm Tue-Sun, to 8:30pm Thu Feb-Oct; ☖; ☐5,6,7,21, Ⓜ Civic Center, Ⓑ Civic Center), enjoy tea-smoked Pacific salmon with soba noodles.

A **B** **C** **D**

WESTERN ADDITION

1

For reviews see
- �‣ Top Sights p98
- ◉ Sights p102
- ✖ Eating p103
- 🍷 Drinking p105
- ★ Entertainment p107
- 🛍 Shopping p109

Eddy St

Ellis St

Gough St

Turk St

Jefferson Square

Golden Gate Ave

Hayward Playground

2

McAllister St

Octavia St

Elm St

Larch St

Franklin St

Buchanan St

Fulton St

Birch St

Laguna St

Grove St

Ivy St

🍷12

Redwood St

McAllister St

3

Hayes St

32 🛍

✖8

🛍 34

Linden St

Patricia's Green

29 15
🛍 🍷
33

Gough St

🛍31

6
✖

War Memorial Opera House

23 21
★★

City Hall

◉2

Dr Carlton B Goodlett Pl

Civic Center Plaza

HAYES VALLEY

🛍27

✖7

★22

Hayes St

★20

Franklin St

Grove St

Ivy St

Van Ness Ave

Page St

Rose St

Haight St

Octavia Blvd

5✖

Fell St

Hickory St

Oak St

19🍷

CIVIC CENTER

4

🛍28
Lily St

19🍷

🍷✖9
16

Market St

Ⓜ Van Ness

McCoppin St

5

Colton St

12th St

11th St

10th St

9th St

30
🛍

Otis St

Mission St

E

F

G

H

Geary Blvd

Hemlock St

26

Cedar St

Polk St

Myrtle St

Van Ness Ave

Olive St

Larkin St

18

24

Willow St

THE
TENDERLOIN

Bush St

Pine St

Sutter St

Post St

Hyde St

Geary St

Leavenworth St

O'Farrell St

11

17

Jones St

Cosmo Pl

Post St

Ellis St

Shannon St

Eddy St

13

Polk St

Larkin St

Hyde St

Turk St

Leavenworth St

Golden Gate Ave

Glide Memorial United
Methodist Church

4

Taylor St

Ellis St

Mason St

Asian Art
Museum

McAllister St

Jones St

Eddy St

3 San Francisco
Main Library

United Nations
Plaza

14

10

25

Powell St
Cable Car
Turnaround

Market St

Civic
Center

8th St

7th St

Stevenson St

Jessie St

6th St

Mission St

1
Luggage
Store
Gallery

UNION
SQUARE

5th St

0   400 m
0   0.2 miles

Sights

Luggage Store Gallery
GALLERY

1 ◎ Map p100, G5

Like a dandelion pushing through sidewalk cracks, this plucky nonprofit gallery has brought signs of life to one of the Tenderloin's toughest blocks for two decades. By giving SF street artists a gallery platform, the Luggage Store helped launch graffiti-art star Barry McGee, muralist Rigo and urban folklorist Clare Rojas. Find the graffitied door and climb to the 2nd-floor gallery, which rises above the street without losing sight of it. (☏415-255-5971; www.luggagestoregallery.org; 1007 Market St; ☉noon-5pm Wed-Sat; ☐5, 6, 7, 21, 31, Ⓜ Civic Center, Ⓑ Civic Center)

City Hall
HISTORIC BUILDING

2 ◎ Map p100, D3

Rising from the ashes of the 1906 earthquake, this beaux arts landmark echoes with history. Singing protesters determined to end red-scare McCarthy hearings were blasted with firehoses here in 1960 – yet America's first sit-in worked. America's first openly gay official Supervisor Harvey Milk was assassinated here in 1978, along with Mayor George Moscone – but in 2004, 4037 same-sex couples were legally wed here for the first time. Lately City Hall has approved pioneering green initiatives, making SF the nation's environmental leader. (☏art exhibit line 415-554-6080, tour info 415-554-6139; http://sfgsa.org/index.aspx?page=1085; 400 Van Ness Ave; admission free; ☉8am-8pm Mon-Fri, tours 10am, noon & 2pm; ☉; Ⓜ Civic Center, Ⓑ Civic Center)

San Francisco Main Library
NOTABLE BUILDING

3 ◎ Map p80, E4

A grand lightwell illuminates San Francisco's favorite subjects: graphic novels in the Teen Center, poetry in the Robert Frost Collection, civil rights in the Hormel Gay & Lesbian Center, and comic relief in the Schmulowitz Wit and Humor Collection. Check out the 2nd-floor wallpaper made from the old card catalog – artists Ann Chamberlain and Ann Hamilton invited 200 San Franciscans to add multilingual commentary to 50,000 cards. The library quietly hosts high-profile basement lectures, plus enlightening Skylight Gallery ephemera exhibits. (☏415-557-4400; www.sfpl.org; 100 Larkin St; ☉10am-6pm Mon & Sat, 9am-8pm Tue-Thu, noon-6pm Fri, noon-5pm Sun; 🛜☉; ☐5, 6, 7, 19, 21, 31, Ⓜ Civic Center, Ⓑ Civic Center)

Glide Memorial United Methodist Church
CHURCH

4 ◎ Map p100, G3

The rainbow-robed Glide gospel choir enters singing their hearts out, and the 2000-plus congregation stomps and dances along. Raucous Sunday Glide celebrations capture San Francisco at its most diverse and welcoming, embracing all ethnicities, abilities and income brackets, the entire LGBT spectrum and many who'd lost all faith in faith. After the celebration ends, the congregation keeps the inspiration coming, serving a million free meals a year and providing housing for 52 formerly homeless families – and yes, Glide welcomes volunteers. (☏415-674-6090; www.glide.org; 330 Ellis St; ☺celebrations 9am & 11am Sun; ♿; ☐38, ⓂPowell, ⒷPowell)

Eating

Rich Table
CALIFORNIAN $$$

5 ☓ Map p100, B4

Satisfy cravings for taste adventures at Rich Table, home of dried porcini doughnuts, octopus confit and totally trippy beet marshmallows. Married co-chefs/owners Sarah and Evan Rich riff on seasonal Californian fare like SFJAZZ masters, hitting their groove with exquisitely playful *amuse-bouches* like the Dirty Hippie: silky goat-buttermilk panna cotta with hemp – a dish as offbeat and entrancing as Hippie Hill drum circles. (☏415-355-9085; http://richtablesf.com; 199 Gough St; mains $12-30; ☺5:30-10pm Sun-Thu, to 10:30pm Fri & Sat; ☐5, 6, 7, 21, 47, 49, ⓂVan Ness)

Jardinière
CALIFORNIAN $$$

6 ☓ Map p100, C3

Iron Chef, Top Chef Master and James Beard Award–winner Traci Des Jardins champions sustainable, salacious California cuisine. She has a way with California's organic produce, sustain-

Warfield (p109)

able meats and seafood that's probably illegal in other states, slathering lamb with mole sauce and pairing velvety sea urchin with satiny lardo. On Monday, $49 scores three courses with wine pairings. (☏415-861-5555; www.jardiniere.com; 300 Grove St; mains $20-35; ☺5-9pm Sun-Thu, to 10pm Fri & Sat; ☐5, 21, 47, 49, ⓂVan Ness)

Nojo
JAPANESE $$

7 ☓ Map p100, C4

Everything you could possibly want skewered and roasted at happy hour, except maybe your boss. Tasting-portion-size Japanese *izakaya* (bar snacks) specialties include grilled chicken *yakitori* (skewers), mushroom-trout surf and turf, and beef tongue slathered in ramp-miso sauce. Local, organic produce brightens every dish; trust staff on wine, beer and sake pairings. (☎415-896-4587; www.nojosf.com; 231 Franklin St; small plates $4-18; ⏱5:30-9:30pm Mon, to 10pm Wed &

Thu, to 10:30pm Fri, 11am-2:30pm & 5:30-10:30pm Sat, 11am-2:30pm & 5-9:30pm Sun; 🚊5, 6, 7, 21, 47, 49, Ⓜ Van Ness)

Souvla
GREEK $

8 Map p100, B3

Ancient Greek philosophers didn't think too hard about lunch, and neither should you at Souvla. Get in line and make no-fail choices: pita or salad, wine or not. Instead of go-to gyros, try roast lamb atop kale with yogurt dressing – or tangy chicken salad with pickled onion and *mizithra* cheese. Go early or late for sky-lit communal seating, or order takeout for Patricia's Green. (☎415-400-5458; 517 Hayes St; sandwiches & salads $12-13; ⏱11am-10pm; 🚊5, 21, 47, 49, Ⓜ Van Ness)

Zuni Cafe
AMERICAN $$$

9 Map p100, B4

Gimmickry is for amateurs – Zuni has been turning basic menu items into gourmet staples since 1979. Reservations and fat wallets are handy for oyster-and-martini lunches, but the see-and-be-seen seating is a kick and simple signatures beyond reproach: Caesar salad with house-cured anchovies, brick-oven-roasted free-range chicken for two with Tuscan bread salad, and mesquite-grilled organic-beef burgers on focaccia (shoestring fries $6 extra). (☎415-552-2522; www.zunicafe.com; 1658 Market St; mains $12-29.50; ⏱11:30am-11pm Tue-Thu, to midnight Fri & Sat, 11am-11pm Sun; 🚊6, 71, 47, 49, Ⓜ Van Ness)

The Hall
FAST FOOD $

10 Map p100, G4

Life is too short to debate lunch – everyone wins at The Hall, lined with tempting options from local purveyors. Check daily menus online – standouts include Little Green Cyclo's organic sirloin *pho* (Vietnamese noodle soup), Fine & Rare's crab Louie salad, Raj & Singh's chickpea samosas, Cassia's coconut-milk braised pork and The Whole Beast's local lamb gyros. Worth braving a sketchy block. (www.thehallsf.com; 1028 Market St; mains $5-14; ⊙11am-8pm Mon-Fri; ⊒6, 7, 9, 21, Ⓜ Civic Center, Ⓑ Civic Center)

farm:table
AMERICAN $

11 Map p100, H2

A ray of sunshine in the concrete heart of the city, this plucky little storefront uses seasonal, regional organics in just-baked breakfasts and farmstead-fresh lunches. Check the daily menu on Twitter (@farmtable) for the savory tart of the day and ever-popular themed pop-ups. Great coffee. Cash only. (☑415-292-7089; www.farmtablesf.com; 754 Post St; dishes $6-9; ⊙7:30am-2pm Tue-Fri, 8am-3pm Sat & Sun; ⊒2, 3, 27, 38)

Drinking

Smuggler's Cove
BAR

12 Map p100, C3

Yo-ho-ho and a bottle of rum...or maybe a Dead Reckoning with Angostura bitters, Nicaraguan rum, tawny port and vanilla liqueur, unless someone will share the flaming Scorpion Bowl? Pirates are bedeviled by choice at this Barbary Coast shipwreck tiki bar, hidden behind a tinted-glass door. With 400-plus rums and 70 cocktails gleaned from rum-running around the world, you won't be dry-docked long. (☑415-869-1900; www.smugglerscovesf.com; 650 Gough St; ⊙5pm-1:15am; ⊒5, 21, 47, 49, Ⓜ Civic Center)

Bourbon & Branch
BAR

13 Map p100, G3

'Don't even think of asking for a cosmo', read the house rules at this revived speakeasy, complete with secret exits from its Prohibition-era heyday. For top-shelf gin and bourbon cocktails in the library, give the bouncer the password ('books') and you'll be led through a bookcase secret passage. Reservations required for front-room booths and Wilson & Wilson Detective Agency, the noir-themed speakeasy-within-a-speakeasy (password supplied with reservations) (☑415-346-1735; www.bourbonandbranch.com; 501 Jones St; ⊙6pm-2am; ⊒27, 38)

Aunt Charlie's Lounge
GAY, CLUB

14 Map p100, G4

Vintage pulp-fiction covers come to life when the Hot Boxxx Girls take the stage at Aunt Charlie's on Friday and Saturday nights at 10pm ($5; call for reservations). Thursday is Tubesteak Connection ($5, free before 10pm), when bathhouse anthems and '80s disco draw throngs of art-school gays. Other nights bring minor mayhem, seedy glamour guaranteed. (☎ 415-441-2922; www.auntcharlieslounge.com; 133 Turk St; cover free-$5; ⏱noon-2am Mon-Fri, from 10am Sat, 10am-midnight Sun; 🚃27, 31, Ⓜ Powell, Ⓑ Powell)

Blue Bottle Coffee Company
CAFÉ

15 🚇 Map p100, B3

Don't mock SF's coffee geekery until you've tried the elixir emerging from this back-alley, garage-door kiosk. The Bay Area's Blue Bottle built its reputation with micro-roasted organic coffee – especially the Blue Bottle–invented,

off-the-menu Gibraltar, the barista-favorite drink of foam and espresso poured together into the eponymous short glass. Expect a wait and seats outside on creatively repurposed traffic curbs. (☎ 415-252-7535; www.bluebottlecoffee.com; 315 Linden St; ⏱7am-6pm; 🚃5, 21, 47, 49, Ⓜ Van Ness)

Hôtel Biron
WINE BAR

16 🚇 Map p100, B4

Duck into the alley to find this walk-in wine closet, with standout Californian, Provençal and Tuscan vintages and a cork-studded ceiling. The vibe is French underground, with exposed-brick walls, surreal romantic art, a leather couch and just a few tables for two. Barkeeps let you keep tasting until you find what you like; pair with decadent cheese and salumi platters. (☎ 415-703-0403; www.hotelbiron.com; 45 Rose St; ⏱5pm-2am; 🚃6, 7, 21, 47, 49, Ⓜ Van Ness)

Rye
LOUNGE

17 🚇 Map p100, G2

Swagger into this sleek sunken lounge for cocktails that look sharp and pack more heat than Steve McQueen in *Bullet*. The soundtrack is '70s soul and the drinks strictly old-school – whiskey sours are stiff with egg whites and drizzled with housemade bitters. Come early to sip at your leisure on leather couches, and leave before the smokers' cage overflows. (☎ 415-474-4448; www.ryesf.com; 688 Geary St; ⏱5:30pm-2am Mon-Fri, from 6pm Sat, from 7pm Sun; 🚃2, 3, 27, 38)

Ⓠ Local Life

Heart of the City Farmers Market

The savviest wheeler-dealers aren't in City Hall – they're over at the **farmers market** (Map p100, E4; www.hotcfarmersmarket.org; United Nations Plaza; ⏱7am-5:30pm Wed, to 5pm Sun; 🚃6, 7, 9, 21, Ⓜ Civic Center, Ⓑ Civic Center), where Californian producers set up shop in the UN Plaza amid the usual skateboarders, Scientologists and raving self-talkers. These stands yield heirloom organic raspberries for $2 a pint and cold-filtered virgin olive oil for $9 a bottle. Off the Grid (p31) food trucks pull up alongside, selling roast chicken with lavender salt and warm maple-bacon doughnuts.

Edinburgh Castle PUB

18 🍺 Map p100, F2

Bagpiper murals on the walls, the *Trainspotting* soundtrack on the jukebox, ale on tap, and a service delivering vinegary fish and chips provide all the Scottish authenticity you could ask for, short of haggis. This bastion of drink comes fully equipped with dartboard, pool tables, and alternating pop-punk and hip-hop DJs on Saturdays. (☎415-885-4074; www.thecastlesf.com; 950 Geary St; ⏱5pm-2am; 🚌19, 38, 47, 49)

Rickshaw Stop CLUB

19 🍷 Map p100, C4

Welcome to the high-school prom you always wanted – theme parties here have been known to bring burlesque trapeze, Brazilian dancers, gypsy brass bands and crowds dressed in drag as dead celebrities. Regular events include Friday night's all-ages (18 plus), Popscene indie bands, monthly Nerd Nite lecture mixers and monthly Cockblock lesbian '90s dance parties. (☎415-861-2011; www.rickshawstop.com; 155 Fell St; cover $5-35; ⏱variable, check website; 🚌21, 47, 49, Ⓜ Van Ness)

Entertainment

San Francisco Symphony CLASSICAL MUSIC

20 ⭐ Map p100, C4

The moment conductor Michael Tilson Thomas bounces up on his toes

Farmers market at United Nations Plaza

and raises his baton, the audience is on the edge of their seats for another thunderous performance by the Grammy-winning SF Symphony. Don't miss signature concerts of Beethoven and Mahler, live Symphony performances with such films as *Star Trek,* and creative collaborations with artists from LeAnn Rimes to Metallica. (☎box office 415-864-6000; www.sfsymphony.org; Grove St, btwn Franklin St & Van Ness Ave; tickets $20-150; 🚌21, 45, 47, Ⓜ Van Ness, Ⓑ Civic Center)

San Francisco Opera OPERA

21 ⭐ Map p100, C3

Opera was SF's Gold Rush soundtrack. Today, SF rivals the Met, with world premieres of original works covering

WWII Italy (*Two Women,* or *La Cioci-ara*), Stephen King thrillers (*Dolores Claiborne*), and Qing Dynasty Chinese courtesans (*Dream of the Red Chamber*). Don't miss Tuscany-born musical director Nicola Liusotti's signature Verdi operas. Score $10 same-day standing-room tickets at 10am and two hours before curtain. (☑415-864-3330; www.sfopera.com; War Memorial Opera House, 301 Van Ness Ave; tickets $10-350; 🚌21, 45, 47, Ⓜ Van Ness, Ⓑ Civic Center)

SFJAZZ Center
JAZZ

22 ⭐ Map p100, C4

Jazz greats coast-to-coast and legends from Argentina to Yemen are showcased at America's newest, largest jazz center. Hear fresh takes on classic jazz albums like *Ah Um* and *Getz/Gilberto* downstairs in the Lab, or book ahead for extraordinary main-stage collabora-tions like Laurie Anderson with David Coulter playing the saw, or pianist Jason Moran's performance with skateboarders improvising moves on indoor ramps. (☑866-920-5299; www.sfjazz.org; 201 Franklin St; tickets $25-120; ⏱showtimes vary; 🚌5, 6, 7, 21, 47, 49, Ⓜ Van Ness)

San Francisco Ballet
DANCE

23 ⭐ Map p100, C3

America's oldest ballet company is looking sharp in more than 100 shows annually, from the *Nutcracker* (the US premiere was here) to modern Mark Morris originals. It performs mostly at War Memorial Opera House January to May, with occasional performances at Yerba Buena Center for the Arts. Score $15 to $20 same-day standing-room tickets at the box office (noon Tuesday to Friday, 10am weekends). (☑tickets 415-865-2000; www.sfballet.org; War Memorial Opera House, 301 Van Ness Ave; tickets $15-160; ⏱ticket sales 10am-4pm Mon-Fri; 🚌5, 21, 47, 49, Ⓜ Van Ness, Ⓑ Civic Center)

Great American Music Hall
LIVE MUSIC

24 ⭐ Map p100, F2

Everyone busts out their best sets at this opulent 1907 former bordello – The Dead occasionally show up, Tuvan throat-singing supergroup Huun Huur Tu throws down and John Waters throws Christmas extravaganzas here. Pay $25 extra for dinner with priority admission and prime balcony seating where you can watch shows

☑ Top Tip

Street Smarts

Most first-time visitors are surprised to find that merely by crossing touristy Powell St or busy Van Ness Ave, they enter the down-and-out Tenderloin. Keep your street smarts about you in the area bounded by Powell and Geary to the north, Mission St to the south and Polk St to the west. When possible, avoid these sketchy blocks, take public transit or cabs through the area, or walk briskly along Geary or Market Sts to reach specific destinations.

comfortably, or enter the standing-room scrum downstairs and rock out on the floor. (☎415-885-0750; www.gamh.com; 859 O'Farrell St; shows $16-26; ⏰box office 10:30am-6pm Mon-Fri & on show nights; 🚍19, 38, 47, 49)

Warfield
LIVE MUSIC

25 ⭐ Map p100, G4

Big acts with international followings play this former vaudeville theater. Marquee names like Wu Tang Clan, Paramore and Nick Cave explain the line down this seedy Tenderloin block and packed, pot-smoky balconies. Beer costs $9 to $10 and water $4, so you might as well get cocktails. Street parking isn't advisable – try the 5th & Mission garage. (☎888-929-7849; www.thewarfieldtheatre.com; 982 Market St; ticket prices vary; ⏰box office 10am-4pm Sun & 90min before shows; Ⓜ Powell; Ⓑ Powell)

Hemlock Tavern
LIVE MUSIC

26 ⭐ Map p100, F1

When you wake up tomorrow with peanut shells in your hair (weren't they on the floor?) and a stiff neck from rocking too hard to Parachute on Fire (weren't they insane?), you'll know it was another successful, near-lethal night at the Hemlock. Blame it on cheap drink at the oval bar, pogo-worthy punk and sociable smoker's room (yes, in California). (☎415-923-0923; www.hemlocktavern.com; 1131 Polk St; cover free-$10; ⏰4pm-2am; 🚍2, 3, 19, 47, 49)

Shopping

Nancy Boy
BEAUTY

27 🔒 Map p100, C3

All you closet pomaders and after-sun balmers: wear those products with pride, without feeling like the dupe of some cosmetics conglomerate. Clever Nancy Boy knows you'd rather pay for the product than for advertising campaigns featuring the starlet du jour, and delivers locally made products with effective plant oils that are tested on boyfriends, never animals. (☎415-552-3636; www.nancyboy.com; 347 Hayes St; ⏰11am-7pm Mon-Sat, to 6pm Sun; 🚍5, 21, 47, 49)

Paloma
ACCESSORIES, GIFTS

28 🔒 Map p100, B4

Like raiding a surrealist's attic, this SF maker collective is a bonanza of unlikely and imaginatively reinvented finds. Don't be surprised to find billiard-ball cocktail rings, or real buffalo nickels on handbags made on-site by artisan Laureano Faedi. For his line of SF-history T-shirts, Laureano unearths insignia for SF's bizarre by-gone businesses, from Playland at the Beach to Topsy's Roost, SF's chicken-coop-themed nightclub. (https://instagram.com/palomahayesvalley; 112 Gough St; ⏰noon-7pm Tue-Sat; 🚍5, 6, 7, 21, 47, 49; Ⓜ Van Ness)

Isotope

COMICS

29 🔒 Map p100, B3

Toilet seats signed by famous cartoonists hang over the front counter, showing just how seriously Isotope takes its comics. Newbies tentatively flip through superhero serials, while fanboys eye new graphic novels from SF's Last Gasp Publishing and head upstairs to lounge with local cartoonists – some of whom teach at Isotope's Comics University. Don't miss signings and epic over-21 after parties. (📞415-621-6543; www.isotopecomics.com; 326 Fell St; ⊙11am-7pm Tue-Fri, to 6pm Sat & Sun; 🚻; 🚌5, 21, 47, 49)

Electric Works

ARTS, BOOKS

30 🔒 Map p100, D5

Everything a museum store aspires to be, with a fascinating collection of arty must-haves – beeswax crayons, East German ice-cream spoons, Klein bottles, vintage wind-up toys – plus limited-edition prints and artists' books by David Byrne, Enrique Chagoya and other contemporary artists. Sales of many artworks printed on-site benefit nonprofits – including Dave Eggers' panda drawing, tragicomically titled *Doomed by Charm*. (📞415-626-5496; www.sfelectricworks.com; 1360 Mission St; ⊙11am-6pm Tue-Fri, to 5pm Sat; 🚻; 🚌14, Ⓜ Van Ness)

MAC

CLOTHING, ACCESSORIES

31 🔒 Map p100, C3

'Modern Appealing Clothing' is what it promises and what it delivers for men and women, with streamlined chic from Maison Martin Margiela, splashy graphic Minä Perhonen shifts and gallery-ready limited-edition tees by developmentally disabled artists at Oakland's Creative Growth. Fashion-savant staff are on your side, finding perfect fits and scores from the 40%-to-75%-off sales rack. (📞415-863-3011; www.modernappealingclothing.com; 387 Grove St; ⊙11am-7pm Mon-Sat, noon-6pm Sun; 🚌5, 21, 47, 49)

Gather

GIFTS, ACCESSORIES

32 🔒 Map p100, B3

For elusive only-in-SF souvenirs to remind you of this singular city, duck into this hidden trove of locally designed and handcrafted finds. Lower Haight drinkers require wooden West Coasters, Zen Center meditators can moisturize thoughtfully with Perfect Harmony lotion, and SF converts scandalize folks back home with Californian-perspective geography tees (Florida's stubby, Seattle's forgotten). Check online for upcoming maker workshops. (📞415-799-7130; www.gathersf.com; 541 Octavia St; ⊙11am-7pm Mon-Sat, to 6pm Sun; 🚌5, 21, 47, 49, Ⓜ Van Ness)

Understand
How Opera Saved San Francisco

At the turn of the 20th century, San Francisco had a reputation for sleaze, scandal and singers. The city commissioned a beaux-arts Civic Center to rival Parisian plazas, including a grand opera. The plan had just been finalized by April 18, 1906, when disaster struck – twice.

A quake estimated at a teeth-rattling 7.8 to 8.3 on today's Richter scale struck. In 47 seconds, San Franciscans discovered just how many corners had been cut on government contracts. Unreinforced civic structures – even City Hall – collapsed in ruins. Since city maintenance funds had been pocketed by unscrupulous officials, fire hydrants didn't work, and there was no way to contain fires. The sole downtown water source was a fountain donated to the city by hometown opera prodigy Lotta Crabtree. The death toll topped 3000; 100,000-plus city residents were left homeless.

With politicians suddenly scarce, San Francisco's entertainers staged the city's comeback. Theater tents were set up amid still-smoking rubble, and opera divas gave marathon free performances. San Francisco hummed along, rebuilding at the astounding rate of 15 buildings a day. In a show of popular priorities, San Francisco's theaters were rebuilt long before City Hall.

Fatted Calf
FOOD & DRINK

33 Map p100, B3

Hostess gifts that win you return invitations to SF dinner parties come from Fatted Calf. This Bay Area salumi maker's showcase is a one-stop shop for California artisan foods, including goat's cheeses, jams and heirloom beans – plus meaty house specialties, from mortadella to duck confit. Don't miss Wednesday Butcher's Happy Hour (5:30om to 7pm) for free bites, drinks and butchery demos. (☑414-400-5614; www.fattedcalf.com; 320 Fell St; ☺10am-8pm; 🚍5, 21, 47, 49, Ⓜ Van Ness)

Marine Layer
CLOTHING

34 Map p100, B3

Get instant California cool without getting the shivers in Marine Layer's 'absurdly soft' tees, which this clever SF company makes from blending cotton and recycled beechwood yarn. That limited-edition 'good vibes' graphic tee designed and manufactured in California makes a feel-good, beach-ready statement – but for Ocean Beach, better add a Marine Layer 'shacket' (heavyweight flannel overshirt) or canvas chore coat. (☑415-829-7519; www.marinelayer.com; 498 Octavia St; ☺10am-7pm; 🚍5, 21, 47, 49, Ⓜ Van Ness)

Explore

The Mission

San Francisco's original neighborhood was built around an 18th-century Spanish mission where nothing seemed to grow, until the Gold Rush brought boatloads of adventurers, and wild speculation took root. The Mission remains fertile ground for vivid imaginations and tall tales told over strong drink – hence mural-lined streets, pirate supplies and literary bar crawls.

The Sights in a Day

 Walk mural-covered, bookstore-lined 24th St to **Balmy Alley** (p118), where the 1970s Mission muralist movement began. Fuel up with **Ritual Coffee Roasters** (p124) coffee and window-shop up Valencia to browse pirate supplies and watch ichthyoid antics in the fish theater at **826 Valencia** (p118).

Duck into **Clarion Alley** (p114) to see the Mission's ongoing outdoor graffiti-art show. Pass muraled **Women's Building** (p115) on your way to **Pizzeria Delfina** (p121) for lunch, or enjoy a **Bi-Rite** (p128) picnic with downtown panoramas on the slopes of **Dolores Park** (pictured left; p115). See San Francisco's first building, Spanish adobe **Mission Dolores** (p118), alongside the memorial to its native Ohlone and Miwok builders.

Check out art shows at **Needles & Pens** (p129) and **Creativity Explored** (p118) before burritos at **Pancho Villa** (p120). Catch an indie movie at the **Roxie Cinema** (p125), then discuss over speakeasy cocktails at **Dalva** (p122).

For a local's day in the Mission, see p114.

Local Life
Sunny Mission Stroll (p114)

Best of San Francisco

Shopping
Gravel & Gold (p127)

Heath Ceramics (p127)

Drinks
Dalva & Hideout (p122)

%ABV (p123)

Elixir (p122)

Entertainment
Roxie Cinema (p125)

Oberlin Dance Collective (p125)

LGBT
El Rio (p123)

Women's Building (p115)

Live Music
The Chapel (p125)

Getting There

B BART Stations at 16th and 24th Sts.

🚌 Bus Bus 14 runs through SoMa to the Mission; 33 links to the Castro; 22 connects to the Haight.

M Streetcar The J Church heads from downtown past Dolores Park.

Local Life
Sunny Mission Stroll

No matter how foggy it gets in Golden Gate Park, San Francisco's mysterious microclimates keep most afternoons sunny in the Mission. Join sun-worship in progress year-round in Dolores Park, line up behind velvet ropes for Bi-Rite ice cream, glimpse what's growing in Dearborn Community Garden and getting graffitied on Clarion Alley, and call it an early happy hour/late lunch at Mission Cheese.

1 Watch Graffiti in Clarion Alley

Most graffiti artists shun broad daylight – but not in **Clarion Alley** (btwn 17th & 18th Sts; off Valencia St; 🚌14, 22, 33, B16th St Mission, MJ), SF's street-art showcase. On sunny days and with prior consent of Clarion Alley Collective, local street artists paint new murals and touch up tagged works. A few pieces survive for years, such as Megan Wilson's daisy-covered *Tax the Rich* or Jet Martinez' glimpse of

Clarion Alley inside a man standing in a forest.

2 Sniff Roses in Dearborn Community Garden

Flowers push through sidewalks elsewhere, but in the Mission, a rogue garden has taken over an entire parking lot. PepsiCo employees once parked on asphalt along Dearborn St, just north of 18th St and west of Valencia St. Neighbors gardened along the edges, but when the Pepsi plant closed in 1991, they got organized. Vegetable plots were planted, property taxes paid and benches installed. Today the garden feeds 40 families, and pleases passersby.

3 Glimpse Goddesses in Women's Building Murals

The nation's first women-owned-and-operated community center has quietly done good work with 170 women's organizations since 1979, but the 1994 *Maestrapeace* mural showed the **Women's Building** (☎415-431-1180; www.womensbuilding.org; 3543 18th St; ♿; ☐14,22,33,49, ᗷ16th St Mission, ᙏJ) for the landmark it truly is. Seven *muralistas* (muralists) and dozens of volunteers covered the building with goddesses and women trailblazers, including Nobel Prize–winner Rigoberta Menchu, poet Audre Lorde and artist Georgia O'Keeffe.

4 Indulge at Bi-Rite Creamery

Velvet ropes at clubs seem pretentious in laid-back San Francisco, but at organic **Bi-Rite Creamery** (☎415-626-5600; www.biritecreamery.com; 3692 18th St; ice cream $3.50-7; ⊙11am-10pm Sun-Thu, to 11pm Fri & Sat; ♿; ☐33, ᗷ16th St Mission, ᙏJ) they make perfect sense. The line wraps around the corner for salted caramel ice cream with housemade hot fudge, or Sonoma honey-lavender ice cream packed into waffle cones. For a quicker fix, get balsamic strawberry soft-serve at the window (1pm to 9pm).

5 Dawdle in Dolores Park

The Mission's living room is **Dolores Park** (http://sfrecpark.org/destination/mission-dolores-park; Dolores St, btwn 18th & 20th Sts; ♿♨; ☐14, 33, 49, ᗷ16th St Mission, ᙏJ), site of semi-professional tanning, free shows and Mayan pyramid playground (sorry kids: no blood sacrifice allowed). Join serious soccer games and lazy Frisbee sessions on flat patches; tennis and basketball courts are open to anyone who's got game. Don't miss downtown panoramas from hillside benches.

6 Mellow Out at Mission Cheese

Wrought-iron dancing skeletons embedded in Valencia St sidewalks mark your path to **Mission Cheese** (☎415-553-8667; www.missioncheese.net; 736 Valencia St; ⊙11am-9pm Tue-Thu & Sun, to 10pm Fri & Sat; ♨; ☐14, 22, 33, 49, ᗷ16th St Mission, ᙏJ). Place your order at the counter, then grab sidewalk seating to gloat over creamy California goat's cheeses, sip Sonoma wines and trend-spot Mission street fashion.

THE MISSION

NOE VALLEY

Dolores Park

26th St
25th St
24th St
23rd St
22nd St
21st St
20th St

Bryant St
Florida St
Alabama St
Harrison St
Treat Ave
Folsom St
Shotwell St
S Van Ness Ave
Capp St
Mission St
Bartlett St
Valencia St
Guerrero St
Ames St
Fair Oaks St
Quane St
Dolores St
Chattanooga St

Cumberland St
Liberty St

8 ✗

19 ❶

Harrison St
Balmy Alley
1 ❶
Lucky St
Treat Ave
Garfield Square
Folsom St
Horace St
Virgil St

34 ❶

28 ❶

Cypress St
Capp St
Lilac St
9 ✗
21 ❶
24th St Mission ❶
5 ✗
16 ▶
Osage St

29 ✗
Orange Al
6 ✗
2 ❶
37 ❶
27 ✗
40 ❶
32 ❶
12 ✗
Poplar St
San Jose Ave
826 Valencia
26 ❶
20 ❶
Elizabeth St

Hill St
Alvarado St
23rd St
24th St
25th St
26th St

Sights

Balmy Alley
MURALS

1 ⊙ Map p116, D7

Inspired by Diego Rivera's 1930s San Francisco murals and outraged by US foreign policy in Central America, 1970s Mission *muralistas* (muralists) set out to transform the political landscape, one mural-covered garage door at a time. Today, Balmy Alley murals span three decades, from an early memorial for El Salvador activist Archbishop Óscar Romero to an homage to Frida Kahlo, Georgia O'Keefe and other trailblazing women modern artists. (☎415-285-2287; www.precitaeyes.org; btwn 24th & 25th Sts; 🚌10, 12, 14, 27, 48, Ⓑ24th St Mission)

○ Local Life
Galería de la Raza

Art flows from Mission streets and across the Americas into **Galería de la Raza** (Map p116, E7; ☎415-826-8009; www.galeriadelaraza.org; 2857 24th St; donations welcome; ⊙during exhibitions noon-6pm Wed-Sat, 1-5pm Tue; 🚼; 🚌10, 14, 33, 48, 49, Ⓑ24th St Mission), a nonprofit Latino art showcase since 1970. Culture and community are constantly being redefined here, from contemporary Mexican photography and group shows exploring Latin gay culture to performances capturing community responses to Mission gentrification.

826 Valencia
CULTURAL SITE

2 ⊙ Map p116, B5

Avast, ye scurvy scalawags! If ye be shipwrecked without yer eye patch or McSweeney's literary anthology, lay down ye dubloons and claim yer booty at this here nonprofit Pirate Store. Below decks, kids be writing tall tales for dark nights a'sea, and ye can study making video games and magazines and suchlike, if that be yer dastardly inclination. Arrrr! (☎415-642-5905; www.826valencia.org; 826 Valencia St; ⊙noon-6pm; 🚼; 🚌14, 33, 49, Ⓑ16th St Mission, ⓂJ)

Creativity Explored
ART GALLERY

3 ⊙ Map p116, A3

Brave new worlds are captured in celebrated artworks destined for museum retrospectives, international shows, and even Marc Jacobs handbags and CB2 pillowcases – all by the local developmentally disabled artists who create at this nonprofit center. Intriguing themes range from monsters to Morse code, and openings are joyous celebrations with the artists, their families and rock-star fan base. (☎415-863-2108; www.creativityexplored.org; 3245 16th St; donations welcome; ⊙10am-3pm Mon-Fri, to 7pm Thu, noon-5pm Sat & Sun; 🚼; 🚌14, 22, 33, 49, Ⓑ16th St Mission, ⓂJ)

Mission Dolores
CHURCH

4 ⊙ Map p116, A3

The city's oldest building and its namesake, whitewashed adobe Misión San Francisco de Asís was founded in 1776

JEREMY GRAHAM / ALAMY ©

and rebuilt in 1782 with conscripted Ohlone and Miwok labor – a graveyard memorial hut commemorates 5000 Ohlone and Miwok laborers who died in mission measles epidemics in 1814 and 1826. Today the modest adobe mission is overshadowed by the ornate adjoining 1913 basilica, featuring stained-glass windows of California's 21 missions. (Misión San Francisco de Asís; 415-621-8203; www.missiondolores.org; 3321 16th St; adult/child $5/3; 9am-4pm Nov-Apr, to 4:30pm May-Oct; 22, 33, B16th St Mission, MJ)

Eating

La Taqueria
MEXICAN $

5 Map p116, C8

SF's definitive burrito has no debatable saffron rice, spinach tortilla or mango salsa – just perfectly grilled meats, slow-cooked beans and classic tomatillo or mesquite salsa wrapped in a flour tortilla. They're purists at La Taqueria – you'll pay extra without beans, because they pack in more meat – but spicy pickles and *crema* (Mexican sour cream) bring complete burrito bliss. (415-285-7117; 2889 Mission St; burritos $6-8; 11am-9pm Mon-Sat, to 8pm Sun; 12, 14, 48, 49, B24th St Mission)

Al's Place
CALIFORNIAN $$

6 Map p116, B8

The Golden State dazzles on Al's plates, featuring homegrown heirloom ingredients, pristine Pacific seafood,

Mission Dolores

and grass-fed meat on the side. Painstaking preparation yields sun-drenched flavors and exquisite textures: crispy-skin cod with frothy preserved-lime dip, creamy grits with goat's-cheese curds and salsa verde. Dishes are half the size but thrice the flavor of mains elsewhere – get two or three, and you'll be California dreaming. (415-416-6136; www.alsplacesf.com; 1499 Valencia St; share plates $13-18; 5:30-10pm Wed-Sun; ; 12,14,49, B24th St Mission, MJ)

Craftsman & Wolves
BAKERY, CALIFORNIAN $

7 Map p116, B4

Conventional breakfasts can't compare to the Rebel Within: savory sausage-spiked Asiago cheese muffin with a silken soft-boiled egg baked inside. SF's surest pick-me-up is Highwire macchiato and matcha (green tea) snickerdoodle cookies, and Thai coconut curry scone, chilled pea soup, and Provence rose makes a sublime lunch. Exquisite hazelnut and *horchata* (cinnamon-rice) cube cakes are ideal for celebrating SF half-birthdays, foggy days and imaginary holidays. (☎415-913-7713;

http://craftsman-wolves.com; 746 Valencia St; pastries $3-7; ⏰7am-7pm Mon-Thu, to 8pm Fri, 8am-8pm Sat, to 7pm Sun; 🚌14, 22, 33, 49, 🚇16th St Mission, Ⓜ J)

La Palma Mexicatessen

GROCERIES $

 8 Map p116, E7

Follow the applause: that's the sound of organic tortilla-making in progress at La Palma. You've found the Mission motherlode of handmade tamales, *pupusas* (tortilla-pockets) with potato and *chicharones* (pork crackling), *carnitas* (slow-roasted pork), *cotija* (Oaxacan cheese) and La Palma's own tangy tomatillo sauce. Get takeout, or bring a small army to finish that massive meal at sunny sidewalk tables. (☎415-647-1500; www.lapalmasf.com; 2884 24th St; ⏰8am-6pm Mon-Sat, to 5pm Sun; 🚇12,14, 27,48, 🚇24th St Mission)

Ichi Sushi

SUSHI $$

9 Map p116, C8

Alluring on the plate and positively obscene on the tongue, Ichi Sushi is a sharp cut above other fish joints. Chef Tim Archuleta slices silky, sustainably sourced fish with a jeweler's precision, balances it atop well-packed rice, and tops it with tiny but powerfully tangy dabs of gelled yuzu and microscopically cut spring onion and chili daikon that make soy sauce unthinkable. (☎415-525-4750; www.ichisushi.com; 3282 Mission Street; sushi $4.50-8.50; ⏰5:30-10pm Mon-Thu, to 11pm Fri & Sat; 🚌14, 24, 49, 🚇24th St Mission, Ⓜ J)

Top Tip

Top Five Mission Tacos

La Palma Mexicatessen *Carnitas* (braised pork shoulder) with pickled red onion on organic tortillas.

Pancho Villa (Map p116, B3; ☎415-864-8840; www.sfpanchovilla.com; 3071 16th St; burritos $5-10; ⏰10am-midnight; 🍴🚹; 🚌14, 22, 33, 49, 🚇16th St Mission) *Pollo verde* (green-chili-stewed chicken) with *escabeche* (spicy pickles).

Namu Gaji Korean steak tacos: grass-fed beef wrapped in seaweed.

Tacolicious (Map p116, B5; ☎415-626-1344; http://tacolicious.com; 741 Valencia St; tacos $4; ⏰11:30am-midnight; 🍴; 🚌14, 22, 33, 49, 🚇16th St Mission, Ⓜ J) Vegetarian taco with roasted squash, peppers and *pepitas* (spiced pumpkin seeds).

La Taqueria (p119) *Lengua* (marinated beef tongue) with pickled jalapeño.

Namu Gaji KOREAN, CALIFORNIAN $$

10 Map p116, A4

SF's unfair culinary advantages – organic local ingredients, Silicon Valley inventiveness and Pacific Rim roots – are showcased in Namu's Korean-inspired soul food. Menu standouts include ultra-savory shiitake mushroom dumplings, meltingly tender marinated beef tongue, and Namu's version of *bibimbap:* Marin Sun Farms grass-fed steak, organic vegetables, spicy *gojuchang* (savorysweet Korean chili sauce) and Sonoma farm egg atop rice, served sizzling in a stone pot. (☏415-431-6268; www.namusf. com; 499 Dolores St; small plates $10-22; ⏱11:30am-3pm Wed-Fri, from 10:30am Sat & Sun, 5-10pm Tue-Thu & Sun, 5-11pm Fri & Sat; ☐14, 22, 33, 49, Ⓑ16th St Mission, ⓂJ)

Pizzeria Delfina PIZZA $$

11 Map p116, A4

One bite explains why SF is obsessed with pizza lately: Delifina's thin crust heroically supports the weight of fennel sausage and fresh mozzarella without drooping or cracking. On sauce-free white pizzas, chefs freestyle with California ingredients such as broccoli rabe, Maitake mushrooms and artisan cheese. No reservations; sign the chalkboard and wait with a glass of wine at next-door Delfina bar. (☏415-437-6800; www.delfinasf.com; 3621 18th St; pizzas $11-17; ⏱11:30am-10pm Tue-Thu, to 11pm Fri, noon-11pm Sat & Sun, 5-10pm Mon; ☐14,22,33,49, Ⓑ16th St Mission, ⓂJ)

Udupi Palace INDIAN $

12 Map p116, B6

Tandoori in the Tenderloin is for novices – SF foodies queue for the bright, clean flavors of Udupi's South Indian *dosa* (light, crispy lentil-flour pancake) dipped in *sambar* (vegetable stew) and coconut chutney. Marathoners may need help finishing a two-foot-long paper *dosa* – save room for pea and onion *utthappam* (lentil-flour pancake) or *bagala bhath* (yogurt rice with nutty toasted mustard seeds). (☏415-970-8000; www. udupipalaceca.com; 1007 Valencia St; mains $8-12; ⏱11:30am-10pm Sun-Thu, to 10:30pm Fri & Sat; ✍; ☐12, 14, 33, 49, Ⓑ24th St Mission)

Chino
CALIFORNIAN, CHINESE $

13 Map p116, B3

San Francisco has been inventing new pseudo-Asian dishes since the Gold Rush – chop suey, anyone? – but Chino's menu is a gold mine of dastardly clever, cheerfully inauthentic Asian soul food. Spicy lamb dumplings get your lips buzzing with Sichuan peppercorns, 'dope-ass Japan-o-Mission wings' with lime hot-and-sour sauce will convert authenticity-trippers, and spiked *boba* (tapioca pearl) cocktails are pure evil genius. (☎415-552-5771; http://chinosf.com; 3198 16th St; share plates $9-14; ☉5-11pm Mon-Thu, to midnight Fri, 11:30am-midnight Sat, 11:30am-11pm Sun; 🚍14,22,49, 🅱16th St Mission, 🅼J)

Local Life
Humphry Slocombe

Indie-rock organic ice cream at **Humphry Slocombe** (Map p116, E7; ☎415-550-6971; www.humphry slocombe.com; 2790 Harrison St; ice cream $4-6; ☉noon-9pm Mon-Thu, to 10pm Fri-Sun; 👶; 🚍12, 14, 49, 🅱24th St Mission) may permanently spoil you for Top 40 flavors. Once Thai Curry Peanut Butter and Magnolia Brewery Stout have rocked your taste buds, cookie dough seems so obvious – and neither sundaes nor salads can compare to Sonoma olive-oil ice cream drizzled with 20-year aged balsamic.

Drinking

Dalva & Hideout
COCKTAIL BAR

14 Map p116, B3

SF's best bars are judged not only by their cocktails, but by the conversations they inspire – and by both measures, Dalva is top-shelf. Discuss Dolores Park doings over Dirty Pigeons (mezcal, lime, grapefruit, gentian-flower bitters), and dissect Roxie documentaries over whiskey cocktails (rye, maraschino, housemade bourbon bitters) in the secret back-room Hideout (from 7pm; cash only). Bargain happy hours last from 4pm to 7pm. (☎415-252-7740; http://dalvasf.com/; 3121 16th St; ☉4pm-2am; 🚍14,22,33,49, 🅱24th St Mission)

Elixir
BAR

15 Map p116, B3

Do the planet a favor and have another drink at SF's first certified-green bar, in an actual 1858 Wild West saloon. Elixir blends farm-fresh seasonal mixers with small-batch, organic, even biodynamic spirits – dastardly tasty organic basil Negronis and kumquat caipirinhas will get you air-guitar-rocking to the killer jukebox. Drink-for-a-cause Wednesdays encourage imbibing, with proceeds supporting local charities. (☎415-522-1633; www.elixirsf.com; 3200 16th St; ☉3pm-2am Mon-Fri, from noon Sat, from 10am Sun; 🚍14,22,33,49, 🅱16th St Mission, 🅼J)

El Rio
CLUB

16 Map p116, C8

Work it all out on the dance floor with SF's most down and funky crowd – SF's full rainbow spectrum of colorful characters is here to party. Calendar highlights include Wednesday's aptly named Mayhem Karaoke, Thursday ping-pong marathons, free oysters Fridays at 5:30pm, and monthly drag-star Daytime Realness. Expect knockout margaritas and shameless flirting in the back garden. Cash only. (415-282-3325; www.elriosf.com; 3158 Mission St; cover free-$8; ⏰1pm-2am; 🚌12, 14, 27, 49, B24th St Mission)

%ABV
BAR

17 Map p116, B3

As kindred spirits will deduce from the name ('percent alcohol by volume'), this bar is backed by cocktail crafters who know their Rittenhouse rye from Traverse City whiskey. Here top-notch hooch is served promptly and without pretension, including historically inspired cocktails under $10. Try toe-warming whiskey concoctions or Lefty's Fizz: mezcal, tart grapefruit shrub and foamy egg white. (415-400-4748; www.abvsf.com; 3174 16th St; ⏰2pm-2am; 🚌14, 22, B16th St Mission, MJ)

Zeitgeist
BAR

18 Map p116, B1

You've got two seconds flat to order from tough-gal barkeeps used to putting macho bikers in their place – but

Roxie Cinema (p125)

with 48 beers on draft, you're spoiled for choice. Epic afternoons unfold in the graveled beer garden, hanging out and smoking at long picnic tables. SF's longest happy hour lasts from 9am to 8pm weekdays. Cash only and no photos (read: no evidence). (415-255-7505; www.zeitgeistsf.com; 199 Valencia St; ⏰9am-2am; 🚌14, 22, 49, B16th St Mission)

Trick Dog
BAR

19 Map p116, E5

Drink adventurously with ingenious cocktails inspired by local obsessions: SF landmarks, Chinese diners, '70s hits, horoscope signs. Every six months, Trick Dog adopts a new theme, and the entire menu changes – proof that you can teach an old dog new tricks, and improve on classics like the Manhattan. Arrive early for bar stools or hit the mood-lit loft for high-concept bar bites. (☏415-471-2999; www.trickdogbar.com; 3010 20th St; ☉3pm-2am; 🚌12, 14, 49)

Ritual Coffee Roasters CAFÉ

20 🎧 Map p116, B6

Cults wish they inspired the same devotion as Ritual, where regulars solemnly queue for house-roasted cap-

---

puccino and specialty drip coffees with highly distinctive flavor profiles – descriptions comparing roasts to grapefruit peel or hazelnut aren't exaggerating. Electrical outlets are limited to encourage conversation, so you can eavesdrop on dates, art debates and political protest plans. (☏415-641-1011; www.ritualroasters.com; 1026 Valencia St; ☉6am-8pm Mon-Thu, to 10pm Fri, 7am-10pm Sat, to 8pm Sun; 🚌14, 49, 🚆24th St Mission)

20 Spot WINE BAR

21 🎧 Map p116, C5

Find your California mellow at this mid-century neighborhood wine lounge. After decades as Force of Habit punk record shop – note the vintage sign – this corner joint has earned the right to unwind with a glass of Californian Gamay noir rosé and not get any guff. Caution: double-deviled eggs with trout roe could become a habit. (☏415-624-3140; www.20spot.com; 3565 20th St; ☉5pm-midnight Mon-Thu, to 1am Fri & Sat; 🚌14, 22, 33, 🚆16th St Mission)

Four Barrel Coffee CAFÉ

22 🎧 Map p116, B2

Surprise: the hippest café in town is also the friendliest, with upbeat baristas and no outlets or wi-fi to hinder conversation. Drip roasts are complex and powerful; the fruity espresso is an acquired taste. The front-bar Slow Pour comes with coffee-geek explanations of growing, roasting and cupping methods. Caffeinating crowds mingle in a sunny parklet with bike parking and patio seating. (☏415-896-

---

4289; www.fourbarrelcoffee.com; 375 Valencia St; ⏰7am-8pm; 🚌14, 22, 33, 49, Ⓑ16th St Mission)

Entertainment

Roxie Cinema
CINEMA

23 ⭐ Map p116, B3

This little neighborhood nonprofit cinema earns international clout for distributing documentaries and showing controversial films banned elsewhere. Tickets to film festival premieres, rare revivals and raucous annual Oscars telecasts sell out – reserve tickets online – but if the main show is packed, check out documentaries in teensy next-door Little Roxie instead. No ads, plus personal introductions to every film. (📞415-863-1087; www.roxie.com; 3117 16th St; regular screening/matinee $10/7.50; ⏰showtimes vary; 🚌14, 22, 33, 49, Ⓑ16th St Mission)

Oberlin Dance Collective
DANCE

24 ⭐ Map p116, C3

For 45 years, ODC has been redefining dance with risky, raw performances and the sheer joy of movement. ODC's season runs September to December, but its stage presents year-round shows featuring local and international artists. ODC Dance Commons is a hub and hangout for the dance community offering 200 classes a week, from flamenco to vogue; all ages and levels welcome. (ODC; 📞box office 415-863-9834, classes 415-549-8519; www.odctheater.org; 3153 17th St;

☑️ Top Tip

Mission Street Smarts

Bars and restaurants make Mission a key nightlife destination, but it's not always the safest area to walk alone at night. Recruit a friend and be alert in the Mission east of Valencia, especially around 19th St gang-turf boundaries. Don't bring the bling – this isn't LA – or dawdle around BART stations. You should be fine in the daytime, but don't leave items like laptops and phones unattended at cafés.

drop-in class $15, shows $20-50; ⏰showtimes vary; 🚌12, 14, 22, 33, 49, Ⓑ16th St Mission)

The Chapel
LIVE MUSIC

25 ⭐ Map p116, B4

Musical prayers are answered in a 1914 California Craftsman landmark with heavenly acoustics. The 40ft roof is raised by shows by New Orleans brass bands, legendary rockers like John Doe, folkYEAH! Americana groups, and AC/DShe, the hard-rocking all-female tribute band. Many shows are all-ages, except when comedians like W Kamau Bell test edgy material. (📞415-551-5157; www.thechapelsf.com; 777 Valencia St; tickets $15-40; ⏰bar 7pm-2am, showtimes vary; 🚌14, 33, Ⓑ16th St Mission, Ⓜ J)

Marsh
THEATER, COMEDY

26 ⭐ Map p116, B6

Choose your seat wisely: you may spend the evening on the edge of it.

One-acts and monologues here involve the audience in the creative process, from comedian W Kamau Bell's riffs to live tapings of NPR's *Philosophy Talk*. A sliding-scale pricing structure allows everyone to participate, and a few reserved seats are sometimes available ($50 per ticket). (📞415-282-3055; www.themarsh.org; 1062 Valencia St; tickets $15-35; ⏰box office 1-4pm Mon-Fri, showtimes vary; 🚊12,14,48,49, **B** 24th St Mission)

Amnesia LIVE MUSIC

27 ⭐ Map p116, B5

Forget everything you've heard about SF nightlife – this closet-sized Boho dive will make you lose your mind for Monday bluegrass jams, Tuesday comedy sessions, Wednesday gaucho jazz, random readings and breakout dance parties. Shows are cheap and often sliding-scale, so the crowd is pumped and the beer flows freely. Check the website or just go with the flow. (📞415-970-0012; www.amnesiathebar.com; 853 Valencia St; cover free-$10; ⏰6pm-2am; 🚊14, 33, 49, **B** 16th St Mission)

Urban Putt MINIATURE GOLF

28 ⭐ Map p116, C6

Leave it to the town that brought you Burning Man and The Exploratorium to make an innocent mini-golf game into a total trip. Urban Putt's course looks like a Tim Burton hallucination, from tricky windmill Transamerica Pyramid Hole 5 to Dia de los Muertos–themed Hole 9. Enjoy big beers with wee snacks, including mini-corndogs, mini-cupcakes and tiny chicken and waffle stacks on sticks. (📞415-341-1080; www.urbanputt.com; 1096 S Van Ness; adult/child $12/8; ⏰4pm-midnight Mon-Thu, to 1am Fri, 11am-1am Sat, 11am-midnight Sun)

Make-Out Room LIVE MUSIC, SPOKEN WORD

29 ⭐ Map p116, C6

Velvet curtains and round booths invite you to settle in for the evening's entertainment, which ranges from punk-rock fiddle to '80s one-hit-wonder DJ mash-ups and painfully funny readings at Writers with Drinks. Booze is a bargain, especially during 6pm-to-8pm weeknight happy hours – but the bar is cash-only. (📞415-647-2888; www.makeoutroom.com; 3225 22nd St; cover free-$10; ⏰6pm-2am; 🚊12, 14, 49, **B** 24th St Mission)

Mission Bowling Club BOWLING

30 ⭐ Map p116, D3

Don't mock it until you try bowling Mission-style: six lanes in a mood-lit warehouse, where the bar pours mean tangerine sours and green-tea gimlets, and $1 of happy hour orders of beef-cheek fries gets donated to local nonprofits. Book lanes in advance online (yes, really) or bide your time for walk-in lanes at the bar. Under-21s allowed only on weekends before 7pm. (📞415-863-2695; www.missionbowlingclub.com; 3176 17th St; ⏰3-11pm Mon-Wed, to midnight Thu & Fri, 11am-midnight Sat, 11am-11pm Sun; 🚊12, 22, 33, 49, **B** 16th St Mission)

Public Works

LIVE MUSIC

31 ⭐ Map p116, C1

Go Public for story-slam nights with NPR's The Moth, afterparties with EDM pioneers The Chemical Brothers, and DJ sets that range from euphoric *bhangra* nights to toga parties where everyone dances like Rome is burning. The on-site Roll Up Gallery encourages SF obsessions with art shows dedicated to Bill Murray, sci-fi and urban flora. (☏415-496-6738; http://publicsf.com; 161 Erie St; ticket prices vary; 🚌14, 49, Ⓑ16th St Mission)

Four Barrel Coffee (p124)

Shopping

Gravel & Gold

CLOTHING, LOCAL ARTISANS

32 🔒 Map p116, B5

Get back to the land and in touch with California's grassroots, without ever leaving sight of a Mission sidewalk. Gravel & Gold celebrates California's hippie homesteader movement with hand-printed smock dresses, trippy totes, and graphic throw pillows. Homestead California-style with hand-thrown stoneware mugs, silkscreened '60s Osborne/Woods ecology posters, and rare books on '70s beach-shack architecture – plus DIY maker workshops (see website). (☏415-552-0112; www.gravelandgold.com; 3266 21st St; ⏱noon-7pm Mon-Sat, to 5pm Sun; 🚌12,14,49, Ⓑ24th St Mission)

Heath Ceramics

HOUSEWARES, LOCAL ARTISAN

33 🔒 Map p116, E4

Odds are your favorite SF meal was served on Heath Ceramics, Bay Area chefs' tableware of choice ever since chef Alice Waters started using Heath's modern, hand-thrown dishes at Chez Panisse. Heath's muted colors and streamlined, mid-century designs stay true to Edith Heath's originals c 1948. New Heath models and factory rejects are sold here; factory tours also available weekends at 11:30am. (☏415-361-5552; www.heathceramics.com; 2900 18th St; ⏱10am-6pm Mon-Wed, Fri & Sat, to 7pm Thu, 11am-6pm Sun; 🚌12,22, 27, 33)

Adobe Books & Backroom Gallery

BOOKS, ART

34 Map p116, D7

Come here for every book you never knew you needed, used and dirt-cheap, plus 'zine launch parties, comedy nights and art openings. Navigate the obstacle course of art books and German philosophy to visit Little Paper Planes artists in residence, and see breakthrough Backroom Gallery shows – artists who debut here often return to Adobe after showing at Whitney Biennials. (☏415-864-3936; www.adobebookshop.com; 3130 24th St; ◷noon-8pm Mon-Fri, from 11am Sat & Sun; ☐12,14,48,49, Ⓑ24th St Mission)

Bi-Rite

FOOD & DRINK

35 Map p116, A4

Diamond counters can't compare to the sheer foodie dazzle of Bi-Rite. Upbeat, knowledgeable staff will help you navigate the brilliant wall of local artisan chocolates, treasure-boxes of organic fruit, and expertly curated Californian wines and cheeses. Step up to the altar-like deli counter to order bespoke sandwiches for five-star Dolores Park picnics. The jawdropping, mouthwatering experience continues at Bi-Rite's second location (500 Divisadero). (☏415-241-9760; www.biritemarket.com; 3639 18th St; sandwiches $7-10; ◷9am-9pm; ♿; ☐14, 22, 33, 49, Ⓑ16th St Mission, ⓂJ)

Aggregate Supply

CLOTHING, GIFTS

36 Map p116, B4

Wild West modern is the look at Aggregate Supply, purveyors of West Coast cool fashion and home decor. Local designers and indie makers get pride of place, including vintage Heath stoneware mugs, Turk+Taylor's ombre plaid shirt-jackets, and ingeniously repurposed rodeo-saddle tassel necklaces. Souvenirs don't get more authentically local than Aggregate Supply's own Op-art California graphic tee and NorCal-forest-scented organic soaps. (☏415-474-3190; www.aggregatesupplysf.com; 806 Valencia St; ◷11am-7pm Mon-Sat, noon-6pm Sun; ☐14, 33, 49, Ⓑ16th St Mission)

Little Paper Planes

LOCAL ARTISANS, ART

37 Map p116, B5

Consider fresh gift possibilities at this purveyor of essential SF oddities: ocean-printed hoodies, SFMOMA-inspired Carrara marble necklaces, eco-friendly glossy black nail polish made in California and self-published manifestos (eg 'Art as a Muscular Principle'). The place is tiny, but thinks big – LPP's artist's residency at Adobe Books yields original works like Hannah Carr's 3D prints, on sale here. (☏415-643-4616; http://littlepaperplanes.com; 855 Valencia St; ◷noon-7pm Mon-Sat, to 6pm Sun; ☐14, 33,49, Ⓑ16th St Mission, ⓂJ)

Needles & Pens   GIFTS, BOOKS

38 Map p116, A3

Do it yourself or DIY trying: this scrappy zine/how-to/art gallery/publisher delivers inspiration to create your own artworks, zines and repurposed fashion statements. Nab limited-edition printings of Xara Thustra's manifesto *Friendship Between Artists Is An Equation of Love and Survival* and H Finn Cunningham's *Mental Health Cookbook* – plus alphabet buttons to pin your own credo onto a handmade messenger bag. (✆415-255-1534; www.needles-pens.com; 3253 16th St; ⏰noon-7pm; 🚌14, 22, 33, 49, **B**16th St Mission)

Nooworks   CLOTHING, LOCAL ARTISANS

39 Map p116, B2

Get a streetwise Mission edge with Nooworks' local-artist-designed fashions, most under $100. Nooworks' evil-eye-print dresses ward off Marina-frat-boy advances, and Muscle Beach maxidresses are Dolores Park–ready, with a psychedelic print of rainbows and flexing bodybuilders that look like California ex-governor Arnold Schwarzenegger. Men's tees featuring cat-headed professors and Ferris Plock's Victorian rowhouses are good to go to any Mission gallery opening. (✆415-829-7623; www.nooworks.com; 395 Valencia St; ⏰11am-7pm Tue-Sat, to 5pm Sun & Mon; 🚌14, 22, 33, 49, **B**16th St Mission)

Tigerlily Perfumery   PERFUME, LOCAL MAKER

40 Map p116, B5

If you just want to bottle San Francisco and take it home with you, you've come to the right place. Tigerlily stocks an intoxicating variety of local perfumers who will transport you from beach days to Barbary Coast nights, from Yosh Han's California-sunbeam scent appropriately called U4EAHH! to Bruno Fazzolari's inky, sultry Lampblack. Check the calendar for in-person perfume events. (✆510-230-7975; www.tigerlilysf.com; 973 Valencia St; ⏰noon-6pm Wed-Thu, 11am-7pm Fri & Sat, noon-5pm Sun; 🚌14, 33, 49, **B**24th St Mission)

Community Thrift   CLOTHING, VINTAGE

41 Map p116, B3

When local collectors and retailers have too much of a good thing, they donate it to Community Thrift, where proceeds go to 200 local nonprofits – all the more reason to gloat over your $5 totem-pole teacup, $10 vintage windbreaker and $14 disco-era glitter romper. Donate your castoffs (until 5pm daily) and show some love to the Community. (✆415-861-4910; www.communitythriftsf.org; 623 Valencia St; ⏰10am-6:30pm; 🚌14, 22, 33, 49, **B**16th St Mission)

Local Life
The History-Making Castro

Within a few years of moving into this quaint Victorian neighborhood in the 1970s, the Castro's out-and-proud community elected Harvey Milk as the nation's first gay official. When AIDS hit, the Castro wiped its tears and got to work, advocating interventions that saved lives worldwide. Today the little neighborhood under the giant rainbow flag is a global symbol of freedom; come out and see for yourself.

Getting There

The Castro is a couple of blocks west of the Mission between 15th and 18th Sts.

Ⓜ Take the scenic above-ground F line from downtown, or underground K, L and M lines.

🚌 Line 33 connects to the Upper Haight and Mission; 24 runs up Divisadero St to the Haight.

1 Come out in Harvey Milk Plaza

A huge, irrepressibly cheerful rainbow flag waves hello as you emerge from the Castro St Muni station into **Harvey Milk Plaza**, and notice the plaque honoring the Castro camera-store-owner turned politician. He was assassinated not long after becoming America's first out gay official, but he's a living symbol of civil rights and civic pride.

2 Toast at Twin Peaks Tavern

A vintage neon rainbow proudly points to **Twin Peaks** (☎415-864-9470; www.twin peakstavern.com; 401 Castro St; ☺noon-2am Mon-Fri, from 8am Sat & Sun; ⓂCastro), the world's first gay bar with windows open to the street. Raise a toast to freedom, watch the gay world go by, and join the inevitable sing-along whenever an '80s anthem hits the jukebox.

3 Walk in the Steps of LGBT Giants

Watch your step on Castro St, or you might step on Virginia Woolf without even realizing it. She's one of 20 pioneering figures featured in bronze sidewalk plaques in the Castro's new **LGBT History Walk of Fame**.

4 Cheer at Castro Theatre

At the deco-fabulous **Castro Theatre** (☎415-621-6120; www.castrotheatre.com; 429 Castro St; adult/child $11/8.50; ☺show-times vary; ⓂCastro), show tunes on a Wurlitzer are overtures to independent cinema, silver-screen gems and live-action drag versions of cult classics.

5 Head Somewhere over the Rainbow

Gay pride stops traffic at Castro and 18th Sts, where crosswalks are rainbow-striped. The southeast corner is a community hub, where protest-ers gather petition signatures, street altars honor bygone community mem-bers and street performers do their thing, often in gold-lamé-thongs.

6 Look Back with Pride

America's first gay-history museum, **GLBT History Museum** (☎415-621-1107; www.glbthistory.org/museum; 4127 18th St; admission $5, 1st Wed of month free; ☺11am-7pm Mon-Sat, noon-5pm Sun; closed Tue fall-spring; ⓂCastro) captures proud moments and historic challenges: Harvey Milk's campaign literature, interviews with trailblazing bisexual author Gore Vidal, matchbooks from long-gone bathhouses and 1950s penal codes banning homosexuality.

7 Think Ahead at Human Rights Campaign Action Center & Store

The storefront home of the **Human Rights Campaign** (http://shop.hrc.org; 575 Castro St; ☺10am-8pm Mon-Sat, to 7pm Sun; ⓂCastro) may look familiar: this was once Harvey Milk's camera shop, as featured in the Academy Award–winning biopic *Milk*. The civil rights advocacy outpost features a stunning mural, 'Equality' wedding rings, and 'Mighty Gay' tees for superheroes with the power to leap out of the closet in a single bound.

Explore

The Haight & NoPa

Was it the fall of 1966 or the winter of '67? As the Haight saying goes, if you can remember the Summer of Love, man, you probably weren't here. But it's not too late to join the revolution at radical cafés and bookstores, or make the scene at Haight and Ashbury Sts – the street corner that became the turning point of the hippie generation.

The Sights in a Day

Start with an eye-opening, rabble-rousing mocha at **Coffee to the People** (p139) before taking the **walking tour** (p162) to spot landmarks from the Haight's hippie heyday, including the heart of the Summer of Love: **Haight & Ashbury** (p136).

After restorative organic pub fare and a homebrew sampler at **Magnolia Brewpub** (p138), try on a few new alter egos on Haight St: Victorian goth at **Loved to Death** (p141), drag diva at **Piedmont Boutique** (p141), manifesto-wielding radical at **Bound Together Anarchist Book Collective** (p141), or decked-out skater at **FTC Skateboarding** (p138).

Along Divisadero St, stroll NoPa (North of the Panhandle) boutiques en route to **Alamo Square** (p136) for breathtaking downtown views behind a jagged Victorian roofline (pictured left). Hit the Lower Haight for sausages from **Rosamunde Sausage Grill** (p137) with microbrews at **Toronado** (p138) – just try not to let the 400-beer selection distract you from showtime at the **Independent** (p139).

 Best of San Francisco

Drinks
Toronado (p138)
Alembic (p139)
Aub Zam Zam (p139)

Shopping
Amoeba Music (p140)
Piedmont Boutique (p141)
Wasteland (p141)
Loved to Death (p141)

Architecture
Alamo Square Park (p136)

Freebies
Concerts at Amoeba Music (p140)

Bargain Gourmet
Rosamunde Sausage Grill (p137)

Live Music
Independent (p139)

Getting There

🚌 **Bus** Lines 6 and 7 run up Haight St; 22 links to the Mission and Marina; 24 to the Castro; 43 to the Marina; 33 to Castro and Golden Gate Park.

Ⓜ **Streetcar** N Judah connects Upper and Lower Haight to downtown and Ocean Beach.

Turk Blvd

Golden Gate Ave

A

B

C

D

Golden Gate Ave

McAllister St

Fulton St

University of
San Francisco

Parker Ave

Fulton St

University
of San
Francisco

Shrader St

Grove St

Cole St

Clayton St

Ashbury St

Masonic Ave

Central Ave

Grove St

Lyon St

Hayes St

Hayes St

2

Fell St

**UPPER
HAIGHT**

3

The Panhandle

Oak St

Lyon St

Page St

Cole St

Haight &
Ashbury

22

9

Haight St

21

17

1

18

Ashbury St

Masonic Ave

20

13

Central Ave

4

10

12

23

14

Shrader St

Waller St

19

Belvedere St

Downey St

3

Grateful Dead
House

**COLE
VALLEY**

Cole St

Buena Vista Ave W

Beulah St

Frederick St

Java St

5

Fulton St

Broderick St

Divisadero St

Scott St

Alamo Square Park
2 ⊙

Grove St

Hayes St

✕
7 ✿16

Fell St

2

🍴15

Fell St

Oak St

LOWER HAIGHT

Oak St

Broderick St

8 ✕

Pierce St

Steiner St

Page St

Fillmore St

3

🍴✕
11 6

Haight St

Baker St

Buena Vista Ave E

Castro St

Scott St

Waller St

Hermann St

Buena Vista Park
⊙
4

Alpine Tce

Divisadero St

Duboce Park

Duboce Ave

4

Park Hill Ave

14th St

Noe St

15th St

Henry St

5

For reviews see

⊙	Sights	p136
✕	Eating	p136
🍴	Drinking	p138
✿	Entertainment	p139
🔒	Shopping	p140

Sights

Haight & Ashbury

LANDMARK

1 ◎ Map p134, C4

This legendary intersection was the epicenter of the psychedelic '60s and remains a counterculture magnet. On an average Saturday here you can sign Green Party petitions, commission a poem, hear Hare Krishna on keyboards and Bob Dylan on banjo. The clock overhead always reads 4:20 – better known in herbal circles as International Bong-Hit Time. A local clockmaker recently fixed it; within a week it was stuck at 4:20. (🚌 6, 7, 33, 37, 43)

Alamo Square Park

PARK

2 ◎ Map p134, G2

The Painted Ladies of famed Postcard Row along the eastern side pale in comparison with the colorful characters along the northwestern end of this 1857 Victorian hilltop park. Alamo Square's north side features Barbary Coast baroque mansions at their most bombastic, bedecked with fish-scale shingles and gingerbread trim dripping from peaked roofs. (www.sfparksalliance.org/our-parks/parks/alamo-square; Hayes & Scott Sts; ☉sunrise-sunset; 🐾; 🚌 5, 21, 22, 24)

Grateful Dead House

NOTABLE BUILDING

3 ◎ Map p134, C5

Like surviving members of the Grateful Dead, this purple Victorian sports a touch of gray – but during the Summer of Love, this was where Jerry Garcia and bandmates blew minds, amps and brain cells. After their 1967 drug bust, the Dead held a press conference here arguing for decriminalization, claiming if everyone who smoked marijuana were arrested, San Francisco would be empty. (710 Ashbury St; 🚌 6, 33, 37, 43, 71)

Buena Vista Park

PARK

4 ◎ Map p134, E4

True to its name, this park founded in 1867 offers splendid vistas over the city to Golden Gate Bridge as a reward for hiking up the steep hill ringed by stately century-old California oaks. Take Buena Vista Ave West downhill to spot Victorian mansions that survived the 1906 earthquake and fire. After-hours boozing or cruising is risky, given petty criminal activity. (http://sfrecpark.org; Haight St, btwn Central Ave & Baker St; ☉sunrise-sunset; 🚌 6, 7, 37, 43)

Eating

Brenda's Meat & Three

SOUTHERN AMERICAN $

5 ✕ Map p134, E1

The name means one meaty main course plus three sides – though only superheroes finish ham steak with Creole red-eye gravy and exemplary grits, let alone cream biscuits and eggs. Chef Brenda Buenviaje's portions are defiantly Southern, which explains brunch lines of marathoners and partiers who forgot to eat last night. Arrive early, share sweet potato pancakes, and pray for crawfish specials. (☎415-926-8657; http://brendasmeatandthree.com; 919 Divisadero St; mains $7-$15; ☺8am-10pm Wed-Mon; 🚍5, 21, 24, 38)

Rosamunde Sausage Grill

FAST FOOD $

6 🍴 Map p134, H3

Impress a dinner date on the cheap: load up classic Brats or duck-fig links with complimentary roasted peppers, grilled onions, whole-grain mustard and mango chutney, and enjoy with your choice of 45 seasonal draft brews at Toronado (p138) next door. To impress a local lunch date, call ahead or line up by 11:30am Tuesdays for massive $6 burgers. (☎415-437-6851; http://rosamundesausagegrill.com; 545 Haight St; sausages $7-7.50; ☺11:30am-10pm Sun-Wed, to 11pm Thu-Sat; 🚍6, 7, 22, Ⓜ N)

Bar Crudo

SEAFOOD $$

7 🍴 Map p134, F2

An international idea that's pure California: seafood served raw Italianstyle, with pan-Asian condiments and East–West beers. Start with Hitachino white ale with velvety avocado-*uni* (sea urchin) toast and graduate to potent Belgian Tripel ales with crudo platters featuring horseradish-spiked Arctic char. Don't miss happy hour (5pm to 6:30pm), when specials include $1 oysters, $6 chowder and $6 wine. (☎415-409-0679; www.barcrudo.com; 655 Divisadero St; share plates $14-22; ☺5-10pm Tue-Thu & Sun, to 11pm Fri & Sat; 🚍5, 6, 7, 21, 24)

EMILY RIDDELL / GETTY IMAGES ©

Toronado (p138)

Ragazza

PIZZA $$

8 🍴 Map p134, F3

'Girl' is what the name means, as in, 'Oooh, *girl*, did you try the wild nettle pizza?!' Artisan salumi is the star of many Ragazza pizzas, from the Amatriciana with pecorino, pancetta and egg to the Moto with Calabrian chili and sausage – best with carafes of Sardinian reds or weighty white Roero Arneis. Arrive early to nab garden patio tables. (☎415-255-1133; www.ragazzasf.com; 311 Divisadero St; pizza $14-19; ☺5-10pm Sun-Thu, to 10:30 Fri & Sat; 👶; 🚍6, 7, 21, 24)

Local Life
Skate the Haight

Never mind the Golden Gate Bridge: for skaters, Haight St is the ultimate SF icon. The downhill slide from Buena Vista Park to the Lower Haight is captured in countless YouTube videos and SF's own *Thrasher* magazine. Gear up with Western Edition decks featuring ramshackle Victorians from **FTC Skateboarding** (Map p134, B4; ☑415-626-0663; www.ftcsf.com; 1632 Haight St; ☺11am-7pm; ☒6, 7, 33, 37, 43, N), and get the latest skinny on SF street skating from skate-pro staff. Roll to the Lower Haight for skater-designed 'Left Coast' hoodies and streetwise art openings at **Upper Playground** (Map p134, H3; ☑415-861-1960; www.upperplayground. com; 220 Fillmore St; ☺noon-7pm; ☒6, 7, 22, N).

Magnolia Brewpub
CALIFORNIAN, AMERICAN **$$**

9 🍴 Map p134, C4

Organic pub grub and homebrew samplers keep conversation flowing at communal tables, while grass-fed Prather Ranch burgers satisfy stoner appetites in booths – it's like the Summer of Love all over again, only with better food. Morning-after brunches of quinoa hash with brewer's yeast are plenty curative, but Cole Porter pints are powerful enough to revive the Grateful Dead. (☑415-864-7468; www.magnoliapub. com; 1398 Haight St; mains $14-26; ☺11am-

midnight Mon-Thu, to 1am Fri, 10am-1am Sat, 10am-midnight Sun; ☒6, 7, 33, 43)

Escape from New York Pizza
PIZZA **$**

10 🍴 Map p134, A4

The Haight's obligatory mid-bender stop for a hot slice. Pesto with roasted garlic and potato will send you blissfully off to carbo-loaded sleep, but the sundried tomato with goat's cheese, artichoke hearts and spinach will recharge you to go another round. Art donated by fans includes signed rocker head shots (hello, Elvis Costello and Metallica) and cartoons by *The Simpsons'* Matt Groening. (☑415-668-5577; www.escapefromnewyorkpizza.com; 1737 Haight St; slices $5-6; ☺11am-midnight Sun-Wed, to 1am Thu, to 2am Fri & Sat; ☒6, 7, 33, 43, N)

Drinking

Toronado
PUB

11 🍺 Map p134, H3

Hallelujah, beer lovers: your prayers have been answered. Be humbled before the chalkboard altar that lists 45-plus beers on tap and hundreds more bottled, including spectacular seasonal microbrews. Bring cash and order sausages from Rosamunde (p137) next door to accompany ale made by Trappist monks. It may get too loud to hear your date, but you'll hear angels sing instead. (☑415-863-2276; www. toronado.com; 547 Haight St; ☺11:30am-2am; ☒6, 7, 22, N)

Alembic BAR

12 Map p134, A4

The tin ceilings are hammered and floors well-stomped, but drinks expertly crafted from 250 specialty spirits aren't made for pounding – hence the 'No Red Bull/No Jägermeister' sign and duck-heart bar snacks. The Southern Exposure (gin, mint, lime, celery juice) smooths overheated Haight arguments (Janis or Jimi?) but the Vow of Silence (rye, cherry liqueur, bitters) renders everyone speechless. (☏415-666-0822; www.alembicbar.com; 1725 Haight St; ⏰4pm-2am Mon-Fri, from noon Sat & Sun; 🚌6, 7, 33, 37, 43, Ⓜ N)

Coffee to the People CAFÉ

13 Map p134, C4

The people united will never be decaffeinated at this radical coffee house – though dairy-free hemp milk and vegan cookies are optional. Grab seats at bumper-sticker-covered tables, admire hippie macramé on the walls and browse consciousness-raising books. But beware the quadruple-shot Freak Out, which has enough fair-trade espresso to revive the Sandinista movement. Free wi-fi. (☏415-626-2435; 1206 Masonic Ave; ⏰6am-7:30pm Mon-Fri, 7am-8pm Sat & Sun; 📶; 🚌6, 33, 37, 43, 71)

Aub Zam Zam BAR

14 Map p134, B4

Arabesque arches, an *Arabian Nights*–style mural, 1930s jazz on the jukebox and top-shelf cocktails at low-shelf prices have brought Bohemian bliss to Haight St since 1941. Legendary founder Bruno used to throw you out for ordering a vodka martini, but he was a softie in the end, bequeathing his beloved bar to regulars who had become friends. Cash only. (☏415-861-2545; 1633 Haight St; ⏰3pm-2am Mon-Fri, 1pm-2am Sat & Sun; 🚌6, 7, 22, 33, 43, Ⓜ N)

Madrone Art Bar BAR

15 Map p134, F2

Expect the unexpected at this Victorian venue with the Burberry plaid Uzi over the bar, rotating art installations and Motown nights featuring the Ike Turner drink special: Hennessy served with a slap. But nothing beats Purple Thriller mash-ups at the monthly Prince vs Michael Jackson party, when the tiny place packs. Acts range from punk-bluegrass to French rock. Cash only. (☏415-241-0202; www.madroneartbar.com; 500 Divisadero St; cover free-$5; ⏰4pm-2am Tue-Sat, 3pm-1:30am Sun; 🚌5, 6, 7, 21, 24)

Entertainment

Independent LIVE MUSIC

16 Map p134, F2

Shows earn street cred at the intimate Independent, featuring indie dreamers (Magnetic Fields, Death Cab for Cutie), rock legends (Meat Puppets, Luscious Jackson), alterna-pop (The Killers, Imagine Dragons) and comedians (Dave Chapelle, Comedians of Comedy). Ventilation is poor, but drinks are cheap –

SABRINA DALBESIO / GETTY IMAGES ©

Amoeba Music

and movie nights offer free shows with a two-drink minimum. (☎415-771-1421; www.theindependentsf.com; 628 Divisadero St; tickets $12-45; ☺box office 11am-6pm Mon-Fri, to 9:30pm show nights; ➡5, 6, 7, 21, 24)

Booksmith   BOOK READINGS

17 ⭐ Map p134, B4

SF is one of America's top three book markets, and visiting authors make the Booksmith a literary destination. Recent readings include Kazuo Ishiguro, *What If?* comic artist Randall Munroe and '60s icon Peter Coyote. Check the website for book swaps and open-bar Shipwreck events, where authors wreck great books with hastily written fan-fiction. Advance book purchases secure

reserved seating. (☎415-863-8688; www.booksmith.com; 1644 Haight St; ☺10am-10pm Mon-Sat, to 8pm Sun; ; ⓜHaight St)

Club Deluxe   JAZZ

18 ⭐ Map p134, C4

Blame it on the bossa nova or the Deluxe Spa Collins (gin, cucumber, ginger, mint, lemon and soda). Admission is either free or $5 for swinging jazz bands, comedy acts and monthly burlesque shows. Expect mood lighting, cats who wear hats well and dames who can swill highballs without losing their matte red lipstick. (☎415-552-6949; www.clubdeluxe.co; 1511 Haight St; cover free-$5; ☺4pm-2am Mon-Fri, 2pm-2am Sat & Sun; ➡6, 7, 33, 37, 43)

Shopping

Amoeba Music   MUSIC

19 🔒 Map p134, A4

Enticements are hardly necessary to lure the masses to the West Coast's most eclectic collection of new and used music and video, but Amoeba offers listening stations, a free zine with uncannily accurate staff reviews, and a free concert series that recently starred Shabazz Palaces, Billy Bragg and Polyphonic Spree – plus a foundation that's saved one million acres of rainforest. (☎415-831-1200; www.amoeba.com; 1855 Haight St; ☺11am-8pm; ➡7, 33, 43, ⓜN)

Bound Together Anarchist Book Collective
BOOKS

20 🔒 Map p134, C4

Since 1976 this volunteer-run, nonprofit anarchist bookstore has kept free thinkers supplied with organic permaculture manuals, prison literature and radical comics, while coordinating the annual spring Anarchist Book Fair and restoring its 'Anarchists of the Americas' storefront mural – makes us tools of the state look like slackers. Hours are impressively regular, but call ahead to be sure. (☏415-431-8355; http://bound togetherbooks.wordpress.com; 1369 Haight St; ⏰11:30am-7:30pm; ☒6, 7, 33, 37, 43)

Wasteland
VINTAGE, CLOTHING

21 🔒 Map p134, B4

The catwalk of thrift, this vintage superstore adds instant style with barely worn Marc Jacobs smock frocks, '70s Missoni sweaters and a steady supply of go-go boots. Hip occasionally verges on hideous with sequined sweaters and '80s power suits, but at reasonable (not necessarily bargain) prices anyone can afford fashion risks. If you've got excess baggage, Wasteland buys clothes noon to 6pm daily. (☏415-863-3150; www.shop wasteland.com; 1660 Haight St; ⏰11am-8pm Mon-Sat, noon-7pm Sun; ☒6, 7, 33, 37, 43, Ⓜ️N)

Piedmont Boutique
CLOTHING, ACCESSORIES

22 🔒 Map p134, C4

'No food, no cell phones, no playing in the boas,' says the sign at the door – but inside, that last rule is gleefully ignored by drag stars, pageant drop-outs, strippers and people who take Halloween dead seriously (read: all SF). Since 1972 Piedmont's signature get-ups have been designed and sewed in SF, so they're not cheap – but those airplane earrings are priceless. (☏415-864-8075; www.piedmontboutique.com; 1452 Haight St; ⏰11am-7pm; ☒6, 7, 33, 37, 43)

Loved to Death
GIFTS, TAXIDERMY

23 🔒 Map p134, B4

Stuffed deer exchange glassy stares with caged baby dolls over rusty dental tools: the signs are ominous, and for sale. Head upstairs for Goth gifts, including Victorian hair lockets and portable last rites kits. Not for the faint of heart, vegans or shutterbugs – no photos allowed, though you might recognize staff from Discovery Channel's *Oddities San Francisco* reality TV show. (☏415-551-1036; www.lovedtodeath.net; 1681 Haight St; ⏰11:30am-7pm Mon-Thu, to 8pm Fri & Sat, noon-7pm Sun; ☒6, 7, 33, 37, 43, Ⓜ️N)

Explore

Golden Gate Park & the Avenues

When other Americans want an extreme experience, they head to San Francisco – but when San Franciscans go to extremes, they end up here. Surfers brave walls of water on blustery Ocean Beach, runners try to keep pace with stampeding bison in Golden Gate Park, and foodies obsessively Instagram adventurous meals in the Sunset or Richmond, the family-friendly neighborhoods along the park.

The Sights in a Day

☀️ Head to **Ocean Beach** (pictured left; p152) early to catch SF's daredevil surfers, then join wetsuited mavericks at **Trouble Coffee** (p156). Model local-designer hoodies at **Mollusk** (p158) before hopping the N Judah to 9th Ave to **San Francisco Botanical Garden** (p152). Hang out with blue butterflies in the rainforest dome at the **California Academy of Sciences** (p146) and visit outer space in **Morrison Planetarium** (p147) before sustainable dim sum lunches in the **Academy Café** (p147).

☼ Globe-trot from Egyptian goddesses to James Turrell light installations in **de Young Museum** (p148), then enjoy a Zen moment in the **Japanese Tea Garden** (p153). Summit Strawberry Hill for views over **Stow Lake** to the Pacific. Next, take bus 44 to buy gifts at **Park Life** (p158), and get the 2 Clement bus to see sculpture and radical comics at the **Legion of Honor** (p152).

🌙 Follow the trailhead from the Legion to end-of-the-world Pacific sunsets. Take the 38 Geary bus toward tropical cocktails at **Trad'r Sam's** (p156), organic Moroccan-Californian feasts at **Aziza** (p153) and foot-stomping folk music at the **Plough & the Stars** (p157).

👁 Top Sights

Golden Gate Park (p144)

California Academy of Sciences (p146)

de Young Museum (p148)

❤️ Best of San Francisco

Outdoors

Golden Gate Park (p144)

Ocean Beach (p152)

Coastal Trail (p154)

San Francisco Botanical Garden (p152)

Japanese Tea Garden (p153)

Museums

Legion of Honor (p152)

Shopping

Mollusk (p158)

Park Life (p158)

Foggy Notion (p157)

Getting There

🚌 **Bus** Buses 1 and 38 run from downtown; 5 and 21 head along the northern edge of the park; 2 runs along Clement St; 71 follows alongside the park to the south.

Ⓜ **Streetcar** The N train runs from downtown.

Top Sights
Golden Gate Park

Everything San Franciscans love is here: free spirits, free music, penguins, paintings, bonsai and buffalo. A stroll through the park covers 150 years of history, from Victorian Conservatory of Flowers past Hippie Hill drum circles to contemplative National AIDS Memorial Grove. Nearby, wave to penguins at California Academy of Sciences, debate art at de Young Museum and find Zen in the Japanese Tea Garden. Stop to sniff magnolias at San Francisco Botanical Garden, boat across Stow Lake and catch free Polo Fields concerts before racing bison into the sunset.

Map p18

www.golden-gate-park.com

Stanyan St to Great Hwy

5, 7, 18, 21, 28, 29, 33, 44,
N

Conservatory of Flowers in Golden Gate Park

Don't Miss

Stow Lake

A park within the park, **Stow Lake** (www.sfrecpark.org; ☉sunrise-sunset; ♿; ☐7,44, Ⓜ︎N) offers waterfall views, picnics in the Taiwanese pagoda and bird-watching on picturesque Strawberry Hill. Pedal boats, rowboats and electric boats are available daily in good weather at the 1946 boathouse. Ghost-hunters come nightly seeking the White Lady – legends claim she's haunted Stow Lake for a century, searching these shores for her lost child.

Polo Fields Concerts

West around Martin Luther King Jr Dr are the Polo Fields, where the 1967 Human Be-In took place and free concerts are still held during **Hardly Strictly Bluegrass** (www.hardlystrictlybluegrass.com). **Outside Lands** (www.sfoutsidelands.com) festival is also held here each August, with tickets selling out in May.

National AIDS Memorial Grove

This tranquil 10-acre living **memorial grove** (☏volunteering & tours 415-765-0497; www.aidsmemorial.org; Bowling Green Dr; admission free; ☉sunrise-sunset; ♿; ☐7,33, 44, Ⓜ︎N) was founded in 1991 to remember millions of individual lives lost to the AIDS epidemic, comfort heartbroken families and communities, and strengthen national resolve for compassionate care and a lasting cure. Volunteer workdays (8:30am to 12:30pm) and free tours (9am to noon) held the third Saturday of each month, March to October.

Children's Playground

Kids have had the run of the park's southeastern end since 1887. Highlights of this historic children's playground include 1970s concrete slides, a new climbing wall and a vintage 1912 carousel (per ride adult/child $2/1; open daily 10am to 4:15pm).

☑ **Top Tips**

▶ Follow your bliss through Golden Gate Park, where great park pastimes range from disc golf and lindy-hopping to model boat regattas and lawn bowling.

▶ Concessions inside top park attractions can add up fast for hungry families. For cheap, quick eats, look for hot-dog carts along John F Kennedy Dr or street-food trucks near the Music Concourse (between de Young Museum and California Academy of Sciences).

✗ **Take a Break**

On the park's western end, Beach Chalet (p155) is a pleasant parkside dining option.

Just outside the park but near several top park attractions, affordable, tasty lunch options include Cinderella Russian Bakery (p154), Manna (p155) and Masala Dosa (p155).

Top Sights
California Academy of Sciences

Leave it to San Francisco to dedicate a glorious four-story landmark entirely to freaks of nature. Architect Renzo Piano's LEED-certified green building houses 40,000 weird and wondrous animals, with an indoor rainforest dome, penguin habitat and underground aquarium capped by a 'living roof' of California wildflowers.

👁 Map p150, G3

📞 415-379-8000

www.calacademy.org

55 Music Concourse Dr

adult/child $34.95/24.95

🕐 9:30am-5pm Mon-Sat, 11am-5pm Sun

🚌 5, 6, 7, 21, 31, 33, 44, Ⓜ N

Steinhart Aquarium at California Academy of Sciences

Don't Miss

Collections
The Academy's tradition of weird science dates from 1853, and today 60 research scientists and thousands of live animals coexist here. Butterflies alight on visitors in the glass rainforest dome, a rare white alligator stalks a mezzanine swamp and penguins paddle the tank in the African Hall.

Steinhart Aquarium
In the basement aquarium, kids duck inside a glass bubble to enter the Eel Forest, find Nemos in the tropical-fish tanks and befriend starfish in the aquatic petting zoo. Premier attractions include the California aquaculture wall, the walk-in tropical fish theater, columns of golden sea dragons and the huge, shy pink Pacific octopus.

Architecture
To make the Academy the world's greenest museum, Pritzker Prize–winning architect Renzo Piano creatively repurposed the original neoclassical facade while adding a 2.5-acre Living Roof, a lofty lawn polka-dotted with wildflowers, solar panels and air vents.

Morrison Planetarium
Glimpse into infinity under the massive digital projection dome, and time travel through billions of years in a half-hour virtual journey.

Wild Nights at the Academy
After the penguins nod off to sleep, the wild rumpus starts at kids-only Academy Sleepovers. At over-21 NightLife Thursdays, rainforest-themed cocktails are served. Book ahead online.

☑ **Top Tips**

▸ Crowds are biggest on weekends, at over-21 Thursday NightLife events (6pm to 10pm) and Academy sleepovers (6pm to 8am; ages five and up). Weekday afternoons are quieter.

▸ Download the Academy Insider iPhone app (free) for a self-guided tour of the Academy's collections.

▸ Avoid $5 surcharges applied during holidays and other peak periods by pre-ordering tickets online.

✕ **Take a Break**

Academy Café offers quick bites made with sustainable ingredients, including responsibly sourced fish and humanely raised meats.

Top Sights
de Young Museum

Follow sculptor Andy Goldsworthy's artificial sidewalk fault line into Herzog & de Meuron's faultlessly sleek, copper-clad building that's oxidizing green to blend into the park. Don't be fooled by the de Young's camouflaged exterior: shows of global arts and crafts boldly broaden artistic horizons, from Oceanic ceremonial masks to James Turrell's Skyspace installation, built into a hill in the sculpture garden.

Map p18

415-750-3600

http://deyoung.famsf.org

50 Hagiwara Tea Garden Dr

adult/child $10/6

9:30am-5:15pm Tue-Sun, to 8:45pm Fri Apr-Nov

5, 7, 44, M N

de Young Museum

Don't Miss

Collection

You can see all the way from contemporary California to ancient Egypt at the globally eclectic de Young. You might spot uncanny similarities between Gerhard Richter's modern squeegee paintings and traditional Afghani rugs from the textile collection's 11,000-plus works. Upstairs, don't miss excellent modern photography and 19th-century Oceanic ceremonial oars, alongside African masks, Meso-American sculpture and meticulous California crafts.

Blockbuster Shows

The de Young's blockbuster basement shows range from Oscar de la Renta gowns to Keith Haring graffiti and JMW Turner seascapes. Crowd-pleasing exhibits of fashion and treasures are consistent with the de Young's mission to showcase global arts and crafts – and art shows here are equally world-class, gorgeously presented and thoughtfully explained.

Architecture

Swiss architects Herzog & de Meuron (of Tate Modern fame) knew better than to compete with Golden Gate Park's scenery. Instead, they drew the seemingly abstract pattern of the de Young's perforated copper cladding from aerial photography of the park. The de Young's 144ft sci-fi armored tower is one architectural feature that's incongruous with the park setting – but access to the tower viewing room is free, and waiting for the elevator by Ruth Asawa's mesmerizing filigreed pods is an unexpected delight.

☑ Top Tips

▶ The de Young offers exceptional freebies: free admission the first Tuesday of each month, free cafe and sculpture garden access, and free visits to the tower viewing platform.

▶ Fridays are an arty party with live music, performances, film premieres and artists-in-residence mingling over cocktails.

▶ The de Young bookstore has a smartly curated selection of one-of-a-kind jewelry, home decor and fashion.

✗ Take a Break

Discuss art over espresso and Guinness cupcakes inside a garage art installation at Hollow (p156).

Head to Golden Gate Park's southern border for Nopalito's (p154) Cal-Mex tacos, cinnamon hot chocolate and oh yes: margaritas.

E F G H

N
0   1 km
0   0.5 miles

Pacific Ave
Washington St
Clay St
Sacramento St
California St

Mountain
Lake Park

Lake St

California St

Iris Ave
Cook St

Clement St

12 21   22   19

Park Presidio Blvd

6 9

15th Ave
16th Ave
17th Ave
18th Ave
19th Ave
20th Ave
21st Ave
22nd Ave

9th Ave
10th Ave
11th Ave
12th Ave

24

Geary Blvd

Spruce Ave
Parker Ave

Arguello Blvd
Palm Ave
Jordan Ave

Anza St

8th Ave
7th Ave
6th Ave
5th Ave
4th Ave
3rd Ave
2nd Ave

Rossi
Playground

University of
San Francisco

7

Balboa St

Turk Blvd

Balboa St

University of
San Francisco

14th Ave

Funston Ave

Cabrillo St

Cabrillo St

Fulton St

Stanyan St

Fulton St

Lloyd
Lake

John F Kennedy Dr

de Young
Museum

Conservatory Dr
Conservatory
of Flowers

4

Oak St

Page St

Stow Lake Dr

Japanese 5
Tea Garden

California
Academy
of Sciences

Lily
Pond

Elk Glen
Lake

Stow
Lake

San Francisco
Botanical Garden

Middle Dr E

Golden
Gate
Park

Kezar Dr

3

Bowling Green Dr

Lincoln Way

Frederick St

Lincoln Way

Hugo St

10

6th Ave
5th Ave

Carl St

Stanyan St

Irving St

15th Ave
14th Ave

Funston Ave

12th Ave

13

Parnassus
Ave

University
of California
San Francisco

17

11

Judah St

10th Ave
11th Ave

25

8th Ave
9th Ave
7th Ave

4

19th Ave
18th Ave
17th Ave
16th Ave

20th Ave
21st Ave
22nd Ave
23rd Ave
24th Ave

Lawton St

5

For reviews see	
◉ Top Sights	p144
◎ Sights	p152
⊗ Eating	p153
◉ Drinking	p155
☆ Entertainment	p157
🔒 Shopping	p157

Sights

Legion of Honor MUSEUM

1 Map p150, B1

A museum as eccentric and illuminating as San Francisco itself, the Legion showcases a wildly eclectic collection ranging from Monet water lilies to John Cage soundscapes, ancient Iraqi ivories to R Crumb comics. Upstairs are blockbuster shows of Old Masters and Impressionists, but don't miss selections from the Legion's Achenbach Foundation of Graphic Arts collection of 90,0000 works on paper, ranging from Rembrandt to Ed Ruscha. (☑415-750-3600; http://legionofhonor.famsf. org; 100 34th Ave; adult/child $10/6, discount with Muni ticket $2, 1st Tue of month free; ☉9:30am-5:15pm Tue-Sun; ⛻; ☒1, 2, 18, 38)

Ocean Beach BEACH

2 Map p150, A4

The sun sets over the Pacific just beyond the fog at this blustery beach. Most days here are too chilly for bikini-clad clambakes, but fine for hardy beachcombers and hardcore surfers braving riptides (casual swimmers beware). Bonfire policies are under review, but they are currently permitted in artist-designed fire pits only; no alcohol allowed. On Ocean Beach's southern end, beachcombers spot sand dollars and 19th-century shipwrecks. Stick to paths in fragile southern dunes, where skittish snowy plover shorebirds shelter in winter. (☑415-561-4323; www.parks

conservancy.org; Great Hwy; ☉sunrise-sunset; ℙ⛻; ☒5, 18, 31, ⓂN)

San Francisco Botanical Garden GARDENS

3 Map p150, F4

There's always something blooming in these 70-acre gardens, which cover a world of vegetation from South African savannah to New Zealand cloud forest. The Garden of Fragrance is designed for appeal to the visually impaired, and the California native-plant section explodes with color when the wildflowers bloom in early spring, right off the redwood trail. Free arboretum tours take place daily; for details, stop by the bookstore inside the entrance. (Strybing Arboretum; ☑415-661-1316; www.strybing.org; 1199 9th Ave; adult/child $7/5, 7:30-9pm daily & 2nd Tue of month free; ☉7:30am-7pm Mar-Sep, to 6pm Oct–mid-Nov & Mar, to 5pm mid-Nov–Jan, last entry 1hr before closing, bookstore 10am-4pm; ⛻; ☒6, 7, 44, ⓂN)

Conservatory of Flowers GARDENS

4 Map p150, G3

Flower power is alive and well at San Francisco's Conservatory of Flowers. This gloriously restored 1878 Victorian greenhouse is home to freaky outer-space orchids, contemplative floating lilies and creepy carnivorous plants gulping down insect lunches. (☑info 415-831-2090; www.conservatoryofflowers. org; 100 John F Kennedy Dr; adult/child $8/2,

Japanese Tea Garden

1st Tue of month free; ⊙10am-4:30pm Tue-Sun; 🚹; 🚌5, 7, 21, 33, Ⓜ️N)

Japanese Tea Garden GARDENS

5 ◉ Map p150, F3

Since 1894, this picturesque 5-acre garden and bonsai grove has blushed with cherry blossoms in spring, turned flaming red with maple leaves in fall, and lost all track of time in the meditative Zen Garden. (📞tea ceremony reservations 415-752-1171; www.japaneseteagardensf.com; 75 Hagiwara Tea Garden Dr; adult/child $8/2, before 10am Mon, Wed & Fri free; ⊙9am-6pm Mar-Oct, to 4:45pm Nov-Feb; 🅿️🚹; 🚌5, 7, 44, Ⓜ️N)

Eating

Aziza MOROCCAN, CALIFORNIAN $$$

6 🍴 Map p150, E2

Chef Mourad Lahlou's inspiration is Moroccan and his ingredients organic Californian, but the flavors are out of this world: Sonoma duck confit melts into caramelized onion inside flaky pastry *basteeya,* while saffron infuses slow-cooked Sonoma lamb atop barley. Chef Mourad's crossroads cuisine wins Michelin stars and *Iron Chef* battles, but pastry chef Melissa Chou's strawberry-fennel pavola is the perfect goodnight kiss. (📞415-752-2222; www.aziza-sf.com; 5800 Geary Blvd; mains $19-29; ⊙5:30-10:30pm Wed-Mon; 🚌1, 2, 29, 31, 38)

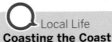

Local Life

Coasting the Coast

Hit your stride on the **Coastal Trail** (Map p150, A1; www.californiacoastaltrail. info; Fort Funston to Golden Gate Bridge; ☉sunrise-sunset; 🚌1, 18, 38) along sandy Ocean Beach, then follow the Presidio coastline to the Golden Gate Bridge. Casual strollers can pick up the trail near Sutro Baths, head around Land's End for end-of-the-world views, then duck into the Legion of Honor at Lincoln Park.

Cinderella Russian Bakery

RUSSIAN $

7 Map p150, G2

Fog banks and cold wars are no match for the heartwarming powers of the Cinderella, serving treats like your babushka used to make since 1953. Join SF's Russian community in Cinderella's new parklet near Golden Gate Park for scrumptious, just-baked egg and green onion *piroshki* pastry, hearty borscht and decadent dumplings – all at neighborly prices. (📞415-751-6723; www.cinderellabakery.com; 436 Balboa St; pastries $1.50-3.50, mains 7-13; ☉7am-7pm; 👶; 🚌5, 21, 31, 33)

Outerlands

CALIFORNIAN $$

8 Map p150, B5

When windy Ocean Beach leaves you feeling shipwrecked, drift into this beach-shack bistro for organic, California coastal comfort food. Brunch demands Dutch pancakes in iron skillets with housemade ricotta, lunch brings $12 grilled artisan cheese combos with surfer-warming soup, and dinner means light, creative coastal fare like clam stew with mezcal broth (hungry surfers: order housebaked levain bread). Reserve ahead. (📞415-661-6140; www.outerlandssf.com; 4001 Judah St; sandwiches & small plates $7-14, mains $18-22; ☉10am-3pm Tue-Fri, from 9am Sat & Sun, 5:30-10pm Tue-Sun; 🍴👶; 🚌18, Ⓜ N)

Dragon Beaux

DIM SUM $$

9 Map p150, E2

Hong Kong meets Vegas at SF's most glamorous, decadent Cantonese restaurant. Say yes to cartloads of succulent roast meats – hello, roast duck and pork belly – and creative dumplings, especially XO dumplings with plump, brandy-laced shrimp in spinach wrappers. Expect premium teas, sharp service and impeccable Cantonese standards, like Chinese doughnuts, *har gow* (shrimp dumplings) and Chinese broccoli in oyster sauce. (📞415-333-8899; www.dragonbeaux.com; 5700 Geary Blvd; dumplings $4-9; ☉11:30am-2:30pm & 5:30-10pm Mon-Thu, to 10:30pm Fri, 10am-3pm & 5:30-10pm Sat & Sun; 👶; 🚌2, 38)

Nopalito

MEXICAN $$

10 Map p150, G4

Head south of Golden Gate Park's border for upscale, sustainably sourced Cal-Mex, including cheesy squash blossom quesadillas with heritage corn tortillas, melt-in-your-mouth *carnitas* (beer-braised pork) and cinnamon-laced Mexican hot chocolate. Reservations aren't accepted, but on sunny weekends when every park-goer craves margaritas and ceviche, call to join the wait list an hour ahead or pre-order online. (📞415-233-9966; www.nopalitosf.com; 1224 9th Ave; mains $11-21; ⏱11:30am-10pm; 🚶♿; 🚌6, 7, 43, 44, Ⓜ N)

Masala Dosa INDIAN $

11 🍴 Map p150, F4

Warm up on Golden Gate Park's southern side with South Indian fare in a mood-lit storefront bistro. The house specialty is paper *dosa,* a massive crispy lentil-flour pancake served with *sambar* (spicy soup) and chutney – but onion and pea *uthappam* is heartier and equally gluten-free. Standout mains include chicken Madras rich with coconut milk and fragrant wild-salmon masala. (📞415-566-6976; www.masaladosasf.com; 1375 9th Ave; dishes $6-14; ⏱11am-11pm; 🚶♿; 🚌6, 7, 33, 43, 44, Ⓜ N)

Spices SICHUAN $

12 🍴 Map p150, G2

The menu reads like an oddly dubbed Hong Kong action flick, with dishes labeled 'fire-burst!!' and 'spicy gangsta' – but peppercorn-infused 'numbing spicy' cucumber, silken 'stinky!' *ma-po* tofu and brain-curdling 'flaming pot' chicken are worthy of exclamation. When you head toward the kitchen for the bathroom, the chili aroma will make your eyes water...or maybe that's just gratitude. Cash only. (📞415-752-8884; http://spicessf.com; 294 8th Ave; mains $7-19; ⏱11am-11pm; 🚌1, 2, 38, 44)

Manna KOREAN $

13 🍴 Map p150, F4

As Korean grandmothers and everyone else who lives in SF's Sunset district will tell you, nothing cures fog chills like home-style Korean cooking. Manna's *kalbi* (barbecue short ribs) and *dol-sot bibimbap* (rice, vegetables, steak and egg in a sizzling stone pot) are surefire toe-warmers, especially with addictive *gojujang* (sweetly spicy Korean chili sauce). Parties of four maximum; expect a wait. (📞415-665-5969; http://mannasf.com; 845 Irving St; mains $10-15; ⏱11am-9:30pm Tue-Sun; 🚌6, 7, 43, 44, Ⓜ N)

Drinking

Beach Chalet BREWERY, BAR

14 🍺 Map p150, A4

Microbrews with views: watch Pacific sunsets through glasses of the Beach Chalet's house beer, with live music most Fridays and Saturdays. Downstairs, splendid 1930s Works Project Administration (WPA) frescoes celebrate the building of Golden Gate Park. The backyard Park Chalet hosts raucous Taco Tuesdays (tacos $3.50), mimosa-fueled Sunday Recovery Brunch Buffets, and Wednesday-to-Friday happy hours (3pm to 6pm). (📞415-386-8439; www.beachchalet.com; 1000 Great Hwy; ⏱9am-10pm Mon-Thu, to 11pm Fri, 8am-11pm Sat & Sun; 🚌5, 18, 31)

Tommy's
Mexican Restaurant
BAR

15 Map p150, D2

Welcome to SF's temple of tequila since 1965. Tommy's serves enchiladas as a cover for day-drinking until 7pm, when margarita pitchers with *blanco, reposado or añejo* tequila rule. Cuervo Gold is displayed 'for educational purposes only' – it doesn't meet Tommy's strict criteria of unadulterated 100% agave, preferably aged in small barrels. Luckily for connoisseurs, 311 tasty tequilas do. (☏415-387-4747; http://tommysmexican.com; 5929 Geary Blvd; ⌚noon-11pm Wed-Mon; ☐1, 29, 31, 38)

Understand
The Fog Belt

Not sure what to wear to a day in Golden Gate Park or dinner in the Avenues? Welcome to San Francisco's fog belt, where coastal fog drops temperatures by up to 20°F (10°C) on the short trip from downtown – you might need a wool coat here in July.

To assess the fog situation, view satellite imagery on the National Oceanic & Atmospheric Administration (NOAA) website (www.wrh.noaa.gov/mtr). When the fog wears out its welcome, head to sunnier spots in the Castro or Mission – or hop BART to sunny Berkeley across the bay.

Trouble Coffee
& Coconut Club
CAFE

16 Map p150, B5

Coconuts are unlikely near blustery Ocean Beach, but here comes Trouble with the 'Build Your Own Damn House' breakfast special: coffee, thick-cut cinnamon toast and an entire young coconut. Join surfers sipping house roasts on driftwood benches outside, or toss back espresso in stoneware cups at the reclaimed wood counter. Featured on NPR, but not Instagram – sorry, no indoor photos. (4033 Judah St; ⌚7am-7pm; ☐18, MN)

Hollow
CAFE

17 Map p150, F4

An enigma wrapped in a mystery inside a garage espresso bar, Hollow serves cultish Ritual coffee and Guinness cupcakes alongside beard conditioner and arsenic-scented perfume. The ideal retreat on foggy Golden Gate Park days, Hollow packs surprisingly ample seating into its snug single-car-garage space – plus arty shopping in the next-door annex that rivals the de Young Museum store. (☏415-242-4119; www.hollowsf.com; 1435 Irving St; ⌚8am-6pm Mon-Fri, from 9am Sat & Sun; ☐7, 28, 29, MN)

Trad'r Sam
BAR

18 Map p150, D2

Island getaways at this vintage tiki dive will make you forget that Ocean Beach chill. Sailor-strength hot but-

tered rum will leave you three sheets to the wind, and five-rum Zombies will leave you wondering what happened to your brain. Kitsch lovers order the Hurricane, which comes with two straws for a reason: drink it solo and it'll blow you away. (📞415-221-0773; 6150 Geary Blvd; ⊙9am-2am; 🚌1, 29, 31, 38)

Entertainment

The Plough & the Stars
LIVE MUSIC

 19 ⭐ Map p150, G2

Bands who sell out shows from Ireland to Appalachia and headline SF's Hardly Strictly Bluegrass festival jam here on weeknights, taking breaks to clink pint glasses of Guinness at long union-hall tables. Mondays compensate for no live music with an all-day happy hour, plus free pool and blarney from regulars; expect modest cover charges ($6 to $14) for barnstorming weekend shows. (📞415-751-1122; www.theploughandstars.com; 116 Clement St; ⊙3pm-2am Mon-Thu, from 2pm Fri-Sun, showtime 9pm; 🚌1, 2, 33, 38, 44)

Balboa Theatre
CINEMA

 20 ⭐ Map p150, C3

First stop, Cannes; next stop, Balboa and 37th, where film-fest favorites split the bill with Chaplin classics, family-friendly Saturday matinees and special screenings with expert commentary – like Spike Jonze's *Her* with Google's

Surfing at Ocean Beach (p152)

artificial intelligence expert. Filmmakers vie for marquee spots at this 1926 movie palace run by nonprofit San Francisco Neighborhood Theater Foundation, which keeps tickets affordable and programming exciting. (📞415-221-8184; www.balboamovies.com; 3630 Balboa St; adult/child $10/7.50; ⊙showtimes vary; ♿; 🚌5, 18, 31, 38)

Shopping

Foggy Notion
GIFTS, ACCESSORIES

21 🔒 Map p150, G2

You can't take Golden Gate Park home with you – the city would seem naked without it – but Foggy Notion specializes in sense memories of SF's urban wilderness. SF's finest all-natural, all-artisan gift selection includes Juniper Ridge's hiking-trail scents, Golden Gate Park honey, SF artist Julia Canwright's handprinted canvas backpacks, and Wildman beard conditioner for scruff soft as fog. (☑415-683-5654; www.foggy-notion.com; 275 6th Ave; ☉11am-7pm Mon-Sat, to 6pm Sun; ☐1, 2, 38, 49)

Top Tip
Freewheeling Through the Park

To cover the entire 48-block stretch of the Golden Gate Park, rent bikes at park-adjacent **San Fran Cyclo** (Map p150, H3; ☑415-831-8031; http://sanfrancyclo.com; 746 Arguello Blvd; rental bicycle per hr $10-35, kid's bicycle/bike seat per day $20, helmet per day $10; ☉11am-7pm Mon-Fri, 10am-5pm Sat & Sun; ⓰; ☐5, 21,31, 33, 38) or skates at **Golden Gate Park Bike & Skate** (Map p150, G3; ☑415-668-1117; www.goldengateparkbikeandskate.com; 3038 Fulton St; skates per hr $5-6, per day $20-24, bikes per hr $3-5, per day $15-25, tandem bikes per hr/day $15/75, discs $6/25; ☉10am-6pm summer, to 7pm winter; ⓰; ☐5, 21, 31, 44). Sundays year-round, Golden Gate Park's John F Kennedy Dr closes to traffic east of Crossover Dr to accommodate cyclists and skaters.

Park Life
ART, GIFTS

22 🔒 Map p150, G2

The Swiss Army knife of hip SF stores: design store, indie publisher and art gallery all in one. It's exceptionally gifted with presents too good to give away, including Golden State pendants, T-shirts for SF's imaginary Aesthetics team, Park Life's catalog of Andrew Schoultz street murals and Anthony Discenza's cryptically cautionary road sign: 'This could be about anything at all.' (☑415-386-7275; www.parklifestore.com; 220 Clement St; ☉11am-8pm Mon-Sat, to 6pm Sun; ☐1, 2, 33, 38, 44)

Mollusk
SURF GEAR

23 🔒 Map p150, B4

The geodesic-dome tugboat marks the spot where ocean meets art in this surf gallery. Legendary shapers (surfboard makers) create limited-edition boards for Mollusk, and signature big wave T-shirts and hoodies win nods of recognition on Ocean Beach. Kooks (newbies) get vicarious big-wave thrills from California surf culture, Thomas Campbell ocean collages and other works by SF surfer-artists. (☑415-564-6300; www.mollusksurf shop.com; 4500 Irving St; ☉10am-6:30pm Mon-Sat, to 6pm Sun; ☐18, Ⓜ N)

Jade Chocolates

FOOD

24 🔒 Map p150, G2

SF-born chocolatier Mindy Fong hits the sweet spot between East and West with only-in-SF treats like passion fruit caramels, jasmine-pearl tea truffles and the legendary peanut Buddha with mango jam. Fusion flavors originally inspired by Fong's pregnancy cravings have won national acclaim, but Jade Chocolates keeps its SF edge with experimental chocolates featuring sriracha, California's homegrown, Asian-inspired chili sauce. (📞415-350-3878; www.jadechocolates.com; 4207 Geary Blvd; ⏰11am-6pm Mon-Sat, 3-6pm Sun; 🚌2, 31, 38, 44)

The Great Overland Book Company

BOOKS

25 🔒 Map p150, G5

SF obsessions go deep at Great Overland, purveyor of rare and obscure books on SF's pet subjects. DIY dandies find inspiration in 1891 *World's Fair Household Companion* recipes for bone-marrow pomade, while bartenders pore over Prohibition pamphlets on making the best of bathtub brandy. For spine-chilling SF history, check out original 1860s Vigilance Committee records and 1949 House Un-American Activities reports. (📞415-664-0126; 345 Judah St; ⏰11am-7pm; 🚌6, 7, 44, Ⓜ N)

🔍 Local Life
Great Park Pastimes

Golden Gate Park (p144) has baseball diamonds, four soccer fields, tennis courts and the vintage-1901 **Lawn Bowling Club** (Map p150, G4; 📞415-487-8787; www.golden-gate-park.com; Bowling Green Dr, Golden Gate Park; ⏰11am-4pm Apr-Oct, from 11am Nov-Mar, weather permitting; 🅿; 🚌5, 7, 21, 33, Ⓜ N), which offers free lessons at noon Wednesdays. Sundays swing at **Lindy in the Park** (Map p150, F3; www.lindyinthepark.com; John F Kennedy Dr, btwn 8th & 10th Aves; admission free; ⏰11am-2pm Sun; ♿; Ⓜ Fulton St), the swing-dance party held outside the de Young Museum. Sporty types conquer the nine-hole **golf course** (Map p150, B4; 📞415-751-8987; www.goldengateparkgolf.com; 970 47th Ave, off Fulton St, Golden Gate Park; adult/child Mon-Thu $17/9, Fri-Sun $21/11; ⏰7am-5pm; ♿; 🚌5, 18, 31) and 18-hole **disc golf course** (Map p150, D3; www.sfdiscgolf.org; Marx Meadow Dr, off Fulton St btwn 25th & 30th Aves; admission free; ⏰sunrise-sunset; 🚌5, 28, 29, 31, 38), while armchair athletes cheer on miniatta regattas at **San Francisco Model Yacht Club** (Map p150, C3; 📞415-386-1037; www.sfmyc.org; Spreckels Lake, Golden Gate Park; ⏰sunrise-sunset; ♿; 🚌5, 18, 31).

The Best of
San Francisco

Cable car, Hyde Street
BUYENLARGE / GETTY IMAGES ©

Best Walks
Haight Flashback

🏃 The Walk

Whether you're a hippie born too late, punk born too early, or a weirdo who passes as normal, Haight St is here to claim you as its own. On this walk you'll cover 100 years of Haight history, starting in 1867 with the park that was San Francisco's saving grace in the disastrous 1906 earthquake and fire. Fog and grit come with the scenery, but there's no better place to break away from the everyday and find your nonconformist niche.

Start Buena Vista Park; 🚇 Haight St

Finish Golden Gate Park; 🚌 Stanyan St

Length 1.3 miles; one hour

🍴 Take a Break

What a long, strange trip it's been – refuel with a burger and beer at **Magnolia Brewpub** (p138), the microbrewery and organic eatery named after a Grateful Dead song.

Hippie Hill, Golden Gate Park

❶ Buena Vista Park

Start your trip back in time in **Buena Vista Park** (p136), where San Franciscans found refuge from the earthquake and fire of 1906, and watched their town burn for three days.

❷ Bound Together Anarchist Book Collective

Heading west up Haight St, you may recognize Emma Goldman and Sacco and Vanzetti in the *Anarchists of Americas* mural at **Bound Together Anarchist Book Collective** (p141). If you don't, staff can provide you with some biographical comics by way of introduction.

❸ SLA Safehouse

At **1235 Masonic Ave**, you might once have glimpsed the Simbionese Liberation Army. Local legend claims this was once a safehouse where the SLA held Patty Hearst, the kidnapped heiress turned revolutionary bank robber.

❹ Grateful Dead House

Pay your respects to the former flophouse of Jerry Garcia, Bob Weir, Pigpen and sundry Deadheads at the **Grateful Dead House** (p136) at 710 Ashbury St. In 1967 cops arrested everyone inside on drug charges. The Dead responded with a press conference, demanding decriminalization.

❺ Janis Joplin's Crash Pad

Down the block, **635 Ashbury St** is one of many Haight addresses for Janis Joplin, who had a hard time hanging onto leases in the 1960s – but as she sang, 'freedom's just another word for nothin' left to lose.'

❻ Haight & Ashbury

At the corner of **Haight & Ashbury** (p136), the clock overhead always reads 4:20, better known in 'Hashbury' as International Bong-Hit Time.

❼ Jimi's Jams

The Victorian at **1524 Haight St** was a notorious hippie flophouse, where Jimi Hendrix crashed in his 'Purple Haze' days. Fittingly, it is now a head shop; the next-door music store sells a lot of guitars.

❽ Hippie Hill

Follow the beat of your own drum to the **Hippie Hill** drum circle in Golden Gate Park – 40 years since it started, free spirits haven't entirely agreed on a rhythm. Notice the shaggy 'Janis Joplin Tree' – squint hard, and it resembles the singer's wild-haired profile.

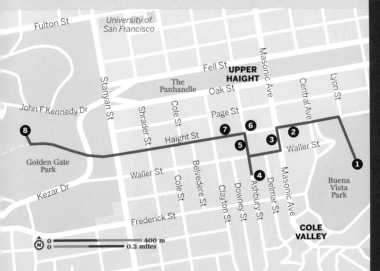

Best Walks
North Beach Beat

🏃 The Walk

Poetry is in the air and on the sidewalk on this literary tour of North Beach featuring legendary City
Lights bookstore, home of Beat poetry and free
speech. It's an easy walk, but you'll want at least a
couple of hours to see the neighborhood as On the
Road author Jack Kerouac did – with drinks at the
beginning, middle and end.

Start Bob Kaufman Alley; 🚌 Columbus Ave

Finish Li Po; 🚌 Kearny St

Length 1.5 miles; two hours

✕ Take a Break

Hot out of the century-old oven, **Liguria Bakery's**
(p61) focaccia is equal parts flour, water and
poetry.

Beat Museum

❶ Bob Kaufman Alley

Quiet Bob Kaufman
Alley is named for the
legendary street-corner
poet who co-founded
Beatitudes magazine in
1959, but took a vow of
silence after Kennedy's
assassination. He didn't
speak again until the
Vietnam War ended,
when he walked into a
North Beach café and
recited 'All Those Ships
that Never Sailed'.

❷ Caffe Trieste

Order a potent espresso,
check out the opera on
the jukebox and slide
into the back booth
under the Sardinian
fishing mural, where
Francis Ford Coppola
drafted *The Godfather*.
Caffe Trieste (p64) has
been a neighborhood
institution since 1956,
with the local characters
and bathroom-wall
poetry to prove it.

❸ City Lights

'Abandon all despair,
all ye who enter,' reads
a sign by poet-founder
Lawrence Ferlinghetti
at **City Lights** (p58).
This commandment is
easy to follow upstairs in
the sunny Poetry Room,

with its piles of freshly published verse. Since winning a landmark free-speech ruling over Allen Ginsberg's *Howl* in 1957, City Lights has published William S Burroughs, Frank O'Hara, Jack Kerouac and Diane di Prima. Rest in the Poet's Chair, and read a poem to inspire your journey through literary North Beach.

❹ Beat Museum

Don't be surprised to hear a Dylan jam session by the front door, or glimpse Allen Ginsberg naked in documentary footage screened inside the **Beat Museum** (p58); the Beat goes on here in rare form.

❺ Specs Museum Cafe

Begin your literary bar crawl at **Specs** (p63) amid merchant-marine memorabilia, tall tales and a glass of Anchor Steam.

❻ Jack Kerouac Alley

On the Road author Jack Kerouac once blew off Henry Miller to go on a bender, until **Vesu-** vio (p66) bartenders ejected him into the street now named for him: **Jack Kerouac Alley** (p59). Note the words of Chinese poet Li Po embedded in the alley: 'In the company of friends, there is never enough wine.'

❼ Li Po Cocktails

Follow the literary lead of Kerouac and Ginsberg and end your night under the laughing Buddha at **Li Po** (p65) – there may not be enough wine among friends, but there's plenty of beer.

Best
Fine Dining

SF FOODPHOTO / GETTY IMAGES ©

Other US cities boast bigger monuments, but San Francisco packs more flavor. With more restaurants per capita than any other North American city (sorry, New York), San Francisco spoils diners for choice. Almost anything grows in California's fertile farmland, so SF's top chefs have an unfair advantage with local, organic, flavor-bursting ingredients.

Wild West Cuisine

Multi-ethnic San Francisco has been finessing fusion since the Gold Rush days, when miners exchanged nuggets for Wild West feasts of oysters, French champagne and Chinese noodles. SF's favorite flavors are still cross-cultural, but now they're homegrown: oysters sustainably farmed in Sonoma, bubbly from Napa, and noodles with California-invented sriracha sauce.

After the 1960s, many disillusioned idealists concluded that the revolution was not about to be delivered on a platter – but chef Alice Waters thought otherwise. In 1971 she opened Chez Panisse in a converted house in Berkeley, with the then-radical notion of highlighting local, seasonal, sustainably produced bounty. Diners tasted the difference for themselves, and today her influence is all over SF menus, from locally foraged morels to certified-humane eggs. SF's sourcing obsessions sound excessive, but it's hard to argue with the results – especially with your mouth full.

Etiquette

SF's top tables are mostly California casual: jeans are acceptable, welcomes warm rather than formal, and servers informative to the point of chatty. Budget

☑ Top Tips

▶ On weekends reservations are usually mandatory, unless you want to eat before 6pm or after 9:30pm.

▶ Most SF restaurants offer online reservations through **OpenTable** (www.opentable.com), but if the system shows no availability, call the restaurant directly. Some seats may be held for phone reservations and walk-ins.

an additional 9.5% for tax, tips ranging from 15% (faulty service) to 25% (exceptional attention). Some restaurants tack on a 4% employee health-care surcharge.

Chez Panisse

Fusion Flair

Benu Fine dining meets DJ styling: ingenious remixes of Eastern classics with the best ingredients in the West. (p84)

Aziza Sunny flavors evaporate Pacific fog in the Avenues, where California bumps up against Morocco. (p153)

Namu Gaji Organic Korean-inspired, Sonoma-grown soul food at communal tables. (p121)

Ichi Sushi Sustainable seafood dressed to impress with California ingredients. (p120)

California's Wild Side

Coi Wild tasting menus featuring foraged morels, wildflowers and Pacific seafood. (p60)

Rich Table Freestyling California fare with French finesse. (p103)

Al's Place California dreaming starts with imaginative plates of pristine Pacific seafood and heirloom NorCal specialties. (p119)

Date-Night Favorites

Boulevard Chef Nancy Oakes' hearty, unfussy Californian fare may be the reason you leave your heart in SF. (p85)

Jardinière Behind the opera, chef Traci Des Jardins hits all the right notes – decadent, smart, sustainable – with a slight Italian accent. (p103)

Gary Danko Escape from Alcatraz for romance served in leisurely, luxuriant courses. (p43)

Worth a Trip

To appreciate the Bay Area's food obsessions, you could read *Slow Food Nation: Why Our Food Should Be Good, Clean and Fair*, by Carlo Petrini and Alice Waters – but it's a pure pleasure to eat her words at **Chez Panisse** (café 510-548-5049, restaurant 510-548-5525; 1517 Shattuck Ave, Berkeley; café dinner mains $19-32, restaurant prix-fixe dinner $75-125; café 11:30am-2:45pm & 5-10:30pm Mon-Thu, 11:30am-3pm & 5-11:30pm Fri & Sat; restaurant seatings 5:30pm & 8pm Mon-Sat). Book ahead.

Best
Bargain Gourmet

Top Chefs for Less

Cotogna Rustic Italian from 2011 James Beard Award–winner Michael Tusk. (p60)

Mijita *Iron Chef* and *Top Chef* Master Traci Des Jardins honors her grandmother's casual Mexican cooking. (p75)

Tout Sweet *Top Chef Desserts* winner Yigit Pura gives French macarons California humor and wit – get the PB&J. (p85)

Food Trucks & Market Stalls

Off the Grid Up to 30 food trucks provide a movable feast, from curry to cupcakes. (p31)

Ferry Plaza Farmers Market Graze on organic peaches, Sonoma goat's cheese and Korean tacos. (p75)

Heart of the City Farmers Market DIY lunches of roast chicken, organic berries, gourmet doughnuts and more. (p106)

The Hall Graze indoors at local mom-and-pop food kiosks, from samosas to gyros. (p105)

Hot Deals

La Taqueria Where SF's most memorable meals come wrapped in foil and under $9 – including spicy pickles. (p119)

Liguria Bakery Foccacia fresh from the century-old oven. (p61)

Z & Y Sichuan specialties poached in flaming chili oil numb lips and blow minds. (p61)

Udupi Palace South Indian in the Mission – SF's definitive *dosa* (lentil pancake). (p121)

Cinderella Russian Bakery Hot *piroshki* (pocket pastries) in a cool parklet. (p154)

Rosamunde Sausage Grill Sausages with free gourmet fixings and next-door microbrews. (p137)

Casual Dates

Outerlands Organic surfer lunches hearty enough to take on big waves. (p154)

Trestle Sweetest deal downtown: three

JUDY BELLAH / GETTY IMAGES ©

☑ **Top Tips**

▶ Track food trucks at **Roaming Hunger** (www.roaminghunger.com/sf/vendors) or on Twitter (@Mobile Cravings/sf-food-trucks, @streetfoodsf).

▶ Deals at top SF restaurants are available at **Blackboard Eats** (http://blackboardeats.com/san-francisco) and during January's **SF Restaurant Week** (www.sfrestaurantweek.com).

tasty courses for $35. (p86)

Dragon Beaux If you're willing to share these brandy-laced XO dumplings, it must be love. (p154)

Best
Live Music

Classical & Opera

San Francisco Symphony Edge-of-your-seat, Grammy-winning performances. (p107)

San Francisco Opera Divas bring down the house with reinvented classics and original works like Stephen King's *Dolores Claiborne*. (p107)

Jazz, Bluegrass & Folk

SFJAZZ Center Top talents reinvent standards and find fresh SF inspiration in mariachis, skateboarding and Hunter S Thompson. (p108)

The Plough & the Stars Major bluegrass and folk bands pack Irish pub benches. (p157)

The Chapel When banjo legends jam with New Orleans brass and Elvis Costello, glory notes hit the rafters of this Craftsman chapel, pictured right. (p125)

Hotel Utah Saloon Twangy indie bands and singer-songwriters get toes tapping in this genuine-article Wild West saloon. (p92)

Rock, R&B & Pop

Great American Music Hall A former bordello now hosts red-hot acts, from alt-rock legends and baroque poppers to world music. (p108)

Slim's From punk to Prince, major acts pack the dance floor at this cozy all-ages venue. (p91)

Warfield Marquee acts get balconies roaring at this former vaudeville theater. (p109)

Bimbo's 365 Club Top 40 names and retro-rockers play a historic speakeasy. (p66)

Independent True to its name, this compact venue features indie dreamers, offbeat comedians and alterna-pop stars. (p139)

Mezzanine Street cred and sound quality – West Coast rap and throwback bands on the comeback trail. (p92)

STEVE JENNINGS / GETTY IMAGES ©

☑ Top Tips

▶ Bargain tickets are sold on the day of the performance for cash only at **TIX Bay Area** (www.tixbayarea.org). Otherwise, try SF-based **Craig's List** (www.craigslist.org).

Best
Drinks

Ban 'the usual' from your drinking vocabulary – you won't find that here. The Gold Rush brought a rush on the bar; by 1850 San Francisco had 500 saloons supplied by local brewers, distillers and Sonoma vineyards. Today California's homegrown traditions of wine, beer and cocktails are converging in saloon revivals, award-winning wines and microbrewery booms – and, for the morning after, specialty coffee roasters.

ROBERT CLAY / ALAMY ©

SF Cocktails – History in the Making

In San Francisco's Barbary Coast days, cocktails were used to sedate sailors and shanghai them onto outbound ships. Now bartenders are researching local recipes and reviving old SF traditions, pouring rye and homemade bitters over hand-hewn ice cubes, whipping egg whites into Pisco sours, and apparently still trying to knock sailors cold with combinations of tawny port and agricole rum served in punch bowls.

If you order a martini, you may get the original, invented-in-SF version: vermouth, gin, bitters, lemon, maraschino cherry and ice. All that authenticity-tripping may sound self-conscious, but after strong pours at California's vintage saloons, consciousness is hardly an issue.

Museums After Hours

Museums offer some of SF's wildest nights out. NightLife at California Academy of Sciences (p146) has rainforest-themed cocktails every Thursday night. Exploratorium (p50) offers mad-scientist glow-in-the-dark cocktails at After Dark events, while the de Young Museum (p148) invites you to mingle with artists-in-residence over art-themed cocktails at first Friday openings.

Beer

Zeitgeist Beer garden with surly lady bartenders tapping 40 microbrews. (p123)

Toronado Beer for every season and any reason – summer ales, holiday barley wines, Oktoberfest wheats. (p138)

Irish Bank Downtown's secret Emerald Isle getaway offers properly poured Guinness and fish and chips in cozy snugs. (p89)

Beach Chalet Microbrews with views of Ocean Beach, WPA murals downstairs, and bands in the backyard. Pictured above. (p155)

Speakeasies

Local Edition This just in: sensational cocktails cause stir in basement of the Hearst newspaper building. (p87)

Smuggler's Cove Roll with the rum punches at this Barbary Coast shipwreck bar hidden behind tinted glass. (p105)

Bourbon & Branch Not since Prohibition have secret passwords and gin knowledge been this handy. (p105)

Dalva & Hideout Hidden back-bar cocktails feature housemade bitters and intriguing names – get the Dirty Pigeon. (p122)

California Wine

Hôtel Biron Walk-in closet wine bar with small, standout selection. (p106)

20 Spot Instant mellow, with Eames rockers, deviled duck eggs and 100 wines. (p124)

West Coast Wine & Cheese Pairing local cheese with 26 California, Oregon and Washington wines by the glass. (p31)

Bluxome Street Winery Sample the latest made-in-SF vintages at this winery's tasting bar. (p90)

Cafés

Caffe Trieste The soul of North Beach: poets,

directors, accordion jams and espresso. (p64)

Ritual Coffee Roasters Heady roasts, local art and seats among burlap coffee bags in a cult roastery-café. (p124)

Sightglass Coffee This SoMa roastery looks industrial but serves small-batch roasts from family farms. (p89)

Blue Bottle Coffee Company The back-alley garage that kicked off the Third Wave coffee roastery craze. (p106)

Saloons

Comstock Saloon Vintage Barbary Coast saloon with potent concoctions and dainty bar bites. (p64)

Elixir Organic, local drinks in a Wild West, green-certified saloon. (p122)

Rickhouse Impeccable bourbon drinks in a chic shotgun-shack setting downtown. (p87)

Drink Think-Tanks

Bar Agricole Valedictorian cocktails, with James Beard accolades and double major in history and rum. (p87)

Interval Lose track of time at this fascinating bar dedicated to 4D thinking, next to a

model 10,000-year clock. (p30)

Trick Dog Every six months the cocktail menu reflects a new SF obsession – landmark buildings, say, or Chinese diners. (p123)

Rye Alcohol alchemy: exact ratios of obscure bitters, small-batch liquor and fresh-squeezed juices. (p106)

Alembic Old Tom gin genius and gourmet bites for aficionados. (p139)

Epic Dives

Specs Museum Cafe Drink like a sailor at this hideaway plastered with Seven Seas mementos. (p63)

Hemlock Tavern Peanuts and punk rock, plus near-impossible trivia nights. (p109)

Edinburgh Castle Literary pub with readings, darts and a thick Scottish accent. (p107)

Lounges

Tosca Cafe Warm up from the inside out with jukebox opera and spiked espresso drinks. (p64)

Aub Zam Zam Persian jazz lounge with bargain cocktails in the Haight. (p139)

Best
Lesbian/Gay/Bi/
Trans SF

Doesn't matter where you're from, who you love or who's your daddy: if you're here and queer, welcome home. Singling out the best places to be out in San Francisco is almost redundant. Though the Castro is a gay hub and the Mission is a magnet for lesbians, the entire city is gay-friendly – hence the number of out elected representatives in City Hall.

LGBT Nightlife

New York Marys may label SF the retirement home of the young – the sidewalks do roll up early – but honey, SF's drag glitter nuns need their beauty rest between throwing Hunky Jesus contests and running for public office. Most thump-thump clubs are concentrated not in the lesbian-magnet Mission or historic gay Castro, but in SoMa warehouses, where dancing queens, playgrrrls and leather scenesters can make some noise. In the 1950s, bars euphemistically designated Sunday afternoons as 'tea dances,' appealing to gay crowds to make money at an otherwise slow time – and Sundays remain SF's busiest.

SF Pride Month

No one shows Pride like San Francisco. The world's most extravagant celebration lasts all of June, kicking off with 200 film screenings at the **San Francisco LGBTQ Film Festival** (www.frameline.org), gearing up with **Dyke March & Pink Party** (www.dykemarch.org) and ending in the joyous, 1.2-million-strong **Lesbian, Gay, Bisexual & Transgender Pride Parade** (www.sfpride.org).

JOHN S LANDER / GETTY IMAGES ©

☑ Top Tips

▶ Enjoy public spankings for local charities on the last Sunday in September at the **Folsom Street Fair** (www.folsomstreetfair.com), a clothing-optional leather fair.

▶ Check out the **Sisters of Perpetual Indulgence** (pictured above; www.thesisters.org) calendar for costumed fundraising extravaganzas, including the Hunky Jesus contest on Easter Sunday.

Classic Bars

Stud Leather bears, art drag, rocker-chick nights and raunchy comedy showcases. (p91)

San Francisco LGBT Pride Parade

Eagle Tavern Landmark SoMa leather rocker bar, as friendly/sleazy as you wanna be. (p88)

Twin Peaks Tavern The first gay bar with windows; now there's a neon rainbow. Toast to progress. (p131)

Women into Women

Cat Club Retro '90s twisted Bondage-a-Go-Go and totally rad '80s Thursdays. (p88)

Rickshaw Stop Something for everyone, SF-style: lesbian disco, Bollywood mash-ups, Latin spice. (p107)

El Rio Oyster happy hours, air hockey, slick DJ mixes and SF's flirtiest patio. (p123)

Dance Clubs

BeatBox Mixed-gender warehouse club where the gays come out to play. (p88)

EndUp Ride the beat from Ghettodisco Saturdays to Monday morning sunrises over the freeway. (p90)

DNA Lounge Known for booty-shaking mash-ups, burlesque, Goth and live acts like Prince. (p92)

Drag

Oasis Drag acts so outrageous, you'll laugh until you cough up glitter. (p91)

Aunt Charlie's Lounge Knock-down, drag-out winner for gender-bending shows and dance-floor freakiness. (p105)

By Day

GLBT History Museum The first gay-history museum in America, in the heart of history-making Castro. (p131)

Dolores Park Sun and cityscapes on a grassy southwest slope nicknamed Gay Beach, plus a playground for families. (p115)

Women's Building Glorious murals crown this community institution. (p115)

Party Supplies

Madame S & Mr S Leather Spiked dog collars, PVC hoods and, oh yes, leather. (p95)

Piedmont Boutique Faux-fur hot pants, glitter leg warmers and a boa... done! (p141)

Best
Museums & Galleries

Museums

de Young Museum
Golden Gate Park's global arts and crafts showcase. (p148)

Asian Art Museum Trip through 6000 years and 4000 miles in an hour, with masterpieces from Mumbai to Tokyo. (p98)

California Academy of Sciences Chase butterflies under the rainforest dome or shuffle with the penguins inside this living museum. (p146)

Exploratorium Trippy hands-on exhibits test scientific theories and blow minds at Pier 15. (p50)

Contemporary Jewish Museum Artworks by Warhol, Houdini, Lou Reed and Gertrude Stein prove great minds don't always think alike. (p82)

SFMOMA Expand horizons with expanded contemporary collections in SF's supersized art museum. (p84)

History

Alcatraz Tour the notorious island prison, from solitary cells to attempted escape routes. (p48)

USS Pampanito Dive into history inside this WWII submarine. (p37)

California Historical Society Museum Gold Rush telegrams, earthquake photos, psychedelic rock posters and other SF ephemera. (p83)

Murals

Coit Tower Murals showing SF during the Great Depression got 26 artists labeled first communists, then national treasures. (p54)

Balmy Alley The Mission muralista movement started here. (p118)

Diego Rivera Gallery The mural maestro pauses to admire SF in progress in this fresco self-portrait. (p42)

Maritime Museum WPA murals of surreal sealife line this monumental hint to sailors in need of a scrub. (p41)

LEONARD ZHUKOVSKY / SHUTTERSTOCK ©

Contemporary Art Galleries

Catharine Clark Gallery See artists make art during earthquakes, unmask KKK members, create sculpture in airplane lavatories. (p124)

49 Geary Four floors of galleries covering all media, from interactive environmental art to classic silver-gelatin photographs. (p84)

Luggage Store Gallery Street art comes in from the cold at this breakthrough art nonprofit. (p102)

Adobe Books & Backroom Gallery Art made on-site by the artist in residence, plus art books and zines galore. (p128)

Electric Works Affordable art multiples and cleverly curated museum shop. (p110)

Best
Architecture

Superman wouldn't be so impressive in San Francisco, where most buildings are small enough for a middling superhero to leap in a single bound. But San Francisco's low-profile buildings are its highlights, from original adobe and gabled Victorians to flower-topped museums.

DEA/W BUSS / GETTY IMAGES ©

Iconic Landmarks

Golden Gate Bridge
Orange deco span with the best disappearing act on the planet. (p24)

Transamerica Pyramid
San Francisco's defining quirk is William Pereira's Egyptian space-age monument, built atop whaling ships. (p83)

Coit Tower The white exclamation point on SF's skyline is dedicated to firefighters and lined with exclamation-worthy murals. (p54)

Palace of Fine Arts
Idealists leap to rescue art atop Bernard Maybeck's romantic neoclassical momument. (p28)

Victorians

Alamo Square Park
Picture-perfect snapshot of SF Victorian architec-

ture, from Queen Annes to Sticks. (p136)

Grateful Dead House
1890 landmark survivor of 1967 police raid. (p136)

Modern Marvels

California Academy of Sciences The world's first Platinum LEED-certified green museum, by Renzo Piano – capped with a living wildflower roof. (p146)

de Young Museum
Herzog & de Meuron's copper-clad building is oxidizing green, blending into park scenery. (p148)

San Francisco Museum of Modern Art Mario Botta's brick-boxed light-well has a radical new extension by Snøhetta architects. (p84)

 **Top Tips**

▶ Stick-style architecture (1870–80s) is characterized by flat fronts and long, narrow windows; see the Mission.

▶ Queen Anne style (1880s–1910) resulted in exuberant turreted, gabled mansions; see the Haight.

▶ Edwardian architecture (1901–14) typically includes false gables and Arts and Crafts details; see the Avenues.

Best
Outdoors

If the climb doesn't take your breath away on San Francisco's hilltop parks, the scenery surely will. Nature has been kind to San Francisco, but it has taken generations of pioneering conservation efforts to preserve this splendor. Early champions include Sierra Club founder John Muir, Golden Gate Park planner William Hammond Hall, and ordinary San Franciscans who saw beauty and not just gold in these hills.

San Francisco's Green Outlook

Recent reports rank San Francisco the greenest city in North America – but you could probably guess that at a glance. All around you'll notice wild ideas at work: mandatory citywide composting, voluntary urban beekeeping, plastic-bag bans and Army airstrips repurposed as nature preserves. This is one town where you can eat, sleep and drink sustainably – and from the bottom of its heart to the top of its green hills, San Francisco thanks you.

Wheels & Waves

Daredevil hills and dazzling waters invite SF visitors to roll, surf and sail around town. Haight St is street-skateboarding at its obstacle-course best, and disco-skaters roll in Golden Gate Park on Sundays.

Bone-chilling Pacific riptides are not for novices; check the **surf report** (☏ 415-273-1618) before you suit up. Sailing is best April through August, but whale-watching season peaks mid-October through December.

BARRY WINIKER / GETTY IMAGES ©

Hilltop Vistas

Coit Tower Parrot's-eye views over the bay along garden-lined stairways, and from the tower's viewing platform. (pictured above; p54)

Alamo Square Park Downtown vistas trimmed with lacy Victorian rooflines. (p136)

Beaches & Waterfront

Crissy Field The retired Army airstrip is now patrolled by windsurfers, shorebirds, joggers and puppies. (p28)

Ocean Beach Beachcombers, surfers and serious sand-castle architects brave SF's blustery Pacific Ocean Beach. (p152)

Crissy Field

Baker Beach Golden Gate Bridge views, sustainable fishing, and clothing-optional sunbathing on a former army base. (p28)

Exploratorium Gauge the bay's mood from pier sensors at the waterfront Bay Observatory. (p50)

San Francisco Maritime National Historic Park Tour 120-year-old boats bobbing like giant bath toys along Fisherman's Wharf. (p38)

Outdoor Activities

Golden Gate Park All of San Francisco's favorite pastimes in one place: baseball, biking, rocking out and lollygagging. (p144)

Coastal Trail Cover 9 miles of waterfront from Fort Funston to Fort Mason, with sparkling Pacific and bay views. (p154)

Dolores Park Serious soccer and hoops, lazy Frisbee and tennis, plus protests, festivals and free summer movies. (p115)

Botanical Wonders

San Francisco Botanical Garden Explore the world inside Golden Gate Park, from California redwoods to South African savannas. (p152)

Japanese Tea Garden Contemplate priceless lost-and-found bonsai over iron pots of tea. (p153)

Urban Wildlife

Sea lions at Pier 39 This harem features more posturing, clowning and in-fighting than a reality TV show. (p37)

Wild parrots at Coit Tower By city decree, SF's official birds are the renegade parrots that turn treetops red, yellow, green and blue around SF's white tower. (p54)

Bison in Golden Gate Park See the smallest stampede in the West run full-tilt toward park windmills. (p144)

Best
Shopping

All those tricked-out dens, well-stocked spice racks and fabulous ensembles don't just pull themselves together – San Franciscans scour their city for them. Eclectic originality is San Francisco's signature style, and that's not one-stop shopping. But consider the thrill of the hunt: while shopping in SF, you can watch fish theater, make necklaces from zippers and trade fashion tips with drag queens.

ROBERT ALEXANDER / GETTY IMAGES ©

Pre-Shopping Planning

Before you browse, check **Urban Daddy** (www.urbandaddy.com) for store openings and events, **Thrillist** (www.thrillist.com) for guy gifts and gadgets, and **Refinery 29** (www.refinery29.com) for sales and trends. Factor nonrefundable SF city and CA state sales taxes into your shopping budget – combined, they tack 8.75% onto purchase prices.

Retail Hotspots

The Marina Date outfits, gifts, wine and design along Union and Chestnut Sts.

Downtown & SoMa Global megabrands and a leather fetish superstore that outsizes Levi's, Gap and Apple flagships.

Russian & Nob Hills Home design, jewelry and designer clothes.

The Mission Local makers, bookstores, art galleries, artisan foods, dandy style, vintage whatever.

The Haight Music, vintage, Goth gifts and skate gear line Haight St.

Hayes Valley Local designers, decor, food and coffee flank Hayes St.

Cali Lifestyle

826 Valencia Pirate supplies to defend SF against scurvy, boredom and Oakland Raiders. (p118)

Gravel & Gold Get good Californian vibrations from G&G's SF-made, feel-good clothing and beach-shack housewares. (p127)

Piedmont Boutique Cross-dress to impress with locally designed drag fabulousness. (p141)

Park Life Instant street smarts, from local-artist-designed tees to original works by SF graffiti artists. (p158)

Little Paper Planes Original gifts by indie makers, gallery-ready clothing and works on paper from LPP's artist's residency program. (p128)

Tigerlily Perfumery Get the scent of Barbary Coast nights and sunny Mission days from local perfumers. (p129)

Local Maker

Heath Ceramics Pottery purveyor to star chefs since 1948. (p127)

Mollusk Surf legends shop here for artist-designed hoodies, T-shirts and hand-shaped surfboards. (p158)

Foggy Notion California chalkboards, Golden Gate Park honey and other SF-made novelties. (p157)

Nancy Boy Overachieving beauty products, locally made with effective natural ingredients. (p109)

SF Fashion Statements

Aggregate Supply Pop-art windbreakers and tees from Turk+Taylor. (p128)

MAC Haute but never haughty: impeccable, easy pieces for trendsetting men and women. (p110)

Harputs Striking sculptural styles good to go from Potrero galleries to SoMa clubs. (p93)

Paloma Leather bags handmade in-store and

historical SF T-shirts. (p109)

Nooworks Eighties New Wave designs reinvented with edgy art-schooled graphics. (p129)

Books

City Lights The landmark bookstore that won a major free-speech lawsuit 50 years ago, and keeps publishing avant-garde literature. (p58)

Adobe Books & Backroom Gallery Readers, cats and art wedged between novels and philosophy. (p128)

The Great Overland Book Company Rare and obscure books on favorite local subjects, from Prohibition gin drinks to Victorian dandy fashion. (p159)

Isotope Browse graphic novels downstairs and read comics upstairs with local cartoonists. (p110)

Needles & Pens Street-art catalogs and hand-stapled zines. (p129)

Vintage

Community Thrift Vintage scores plus store-donated items, with all proceeds going to local charities. (p129)

Wasteland Fashion-forward, retro '40s to

'80s clothes, plus recent designer scores. (p141)

Loved to Death Creepy Victorian hair lockets and pets taxidermied decades ago. (p141)

Gourmet Gifts

Recchiuti Chocolates Local artisan chocolates for every SF occasion, from gourmet brunches to beer tastings. (p94)

Bi-Rite Caution: gazing too long at Bi-Rite's dazzling wines, cheeses and sustainable meats may induce vows to relocate. (p128)

Golden Gate Fortune Cookie Company Make a fortune in San Francisco for 50¢: slip your secret message into a hot cookie here. (p68)

Jade Chocolates Fusion-flavor chocolates hit the sweet spot between East and West. (p159)

Music

101 Music Join DJs thumbing through milk crates of rare, cheap LPs, and you might spot Carlos Santana browsing guitars. (p68)

Amoeba Music Free concerts and a store zine that outsmarts *Rolling Stone*, plus thousands of new and used CDs and DVDs. (p140)

Best For Kids

San Francisco has fewer kids per capita than any US city, and according to SFSPCA data, about 20,000 more dogs than children live here. Yet many locals make a living entertaining kids – from Pixar animators to video-game designers – and this town is packed with childish delights.

KRIS DAVIDSON / GETTY IMAGES ©

Junior Foodies

Discerning young diners can take their pick of dainty dim sum at City View (p62) or food-truck gourmet options at Off the Grid (p31). For foodie prodigies, 18 Reasons (p121) offers classes on pickles and stinky cheeses, Humphry Slocombe (p122) has freaky ice-cream flavors, and the Ferry Building (p74) lets kids graze farm-fresh, top-chef fare.

Major Thrills

Exploratorium Dare you to try these mad-scientist experiments for yourself... (p50)

Cable cars Look, Mom, no seat belt! (p76)

Musée Mécanique Coin-operated saloon brawls, public executions, Pac-Man and other vintage arcade games. (p37)

Alcatraz Spooky sunset tours of the island prison keep kids on best behavior for weeks. (p48)

Dolores Park Slide down a Mayan pyramid to your picnic table. (p115)

Creative Kids

Children's Creativity Museum Live-action video games and kids' claymation workshops taught by special-effects pros. (p82)

826 Valencia Writing workshops, pirate supplies and fish theater spark active imaginations. (p118)

Kids Gone Wild

California Academy of Sciences Penguins, an eel forest, starfish petting zoos and sleepovers amid rare wildlife. (p146)

Sea lions at Pier 39 Bark back at sea lions lazing around the yacht marina. (p37)

Aquarium of the Bay Walk underwater through glass tubes, as skates flutter past and sharks circle around. (p38)

Best
Freebies

Free SF History

Coit Tower Free tours on Wednesday and Saturday mornings cover SF history-redefining murals – including secret stairway gems. (p54)

Rincon Annex Post Office Murals cover San Francisco history, from Native American oyster-gathering origins to McCarthy-era censorship. (p85)

Diego Rivera's Lunch Club Murals See 1930s California through the eyes of the master Mexican muralist at SF's former Stock Exchange Lunch Club. (p82)

Balmy Alley Diego Rivera–inspired Mission garage-door murals, from the 1970s to today. (p118)

Beach Chalet Downstairs lobby lined with uplifting Depression-era murals depicting Golden Gate Park history. (p155)

San Francisco Main Library Volunteer-run neighborhood history walking tours (www.sfcityguides.org) and free on-site history exhibits. (p191)

Maritime Museum Ship-shaped 1939 landmark decked out with mosaics and sculpture by African American modernist Sargent Johnson. (p41)

City Hall Free docent-led tours show where the first sit-in happened, and the first gay official was elected...and assassinated. (p102)

Free Art Shows

Clarion Alley The Mission's open-air graffiti gallery constantly unveils new public artworks. (p114)

49 Geary Free contemporary art shows across four floors, plus free wine on the first Thursday evening of each month. (p84)

Catharine Clark Gallery Bold art banned elsewhere is shown here, and it's free for all. (p124)

Luggage Store Gallery Street artists earn mu-

DEA/W BUSS / GETTY IMAGES ©

seum cred at this urban art nonprofit. (p102)

Free Entertainment

Concerts at Amoeba Music From Elvis Costello to Lana Del Ray, everyone plays free in the back of this music store. (p140)

Dolores Park summer movies Family-friendly fare, especially movies set in SF – expect snark about Mrs Doubtfire's drag. (p115)

Giants games glimpsed from Waterfront Promenade The local crowd may grant you a spot, especially if you bring beer. (p92)

Sea lions at Pier 39 Sea-mammal slapstick on yacht marina docks. (p37)

Best
Entertainment

Theater & Comedy

American Conservatory Theater Breakthrough premieres and provocative original plays, from Tony Kushner to David Mamet. (p90)

Magic Theatre Cutting-edge theater inside a creatively repurposed waterfront army base. (p32)

Cobb's Comedy Club HBO and NBC talents try their riskiest material here first. (p66)

Beach Blanket Babylon Disney drag satire with giant hats and no mercy – a true San Francisco treat. (p66)

Dance

Yerba Buena Center for the Arts Inspirations range from machinery to martial arts at this all-star performing arts showcase. (p93)

Oberlin Dance Collective Raw and risky performances September to December, and 200 dance classes a week year-round. (p125)

San Francisco Ballet
Classical elegance and gorgeous staging, with performances January to May. (p108)

Cinema

Castro Theatre Deco movie palace featuring silver-screen classics and cult hits for cinemaniac audiences. (p131)

Roxie Cinema Film festivals, documentaries and rare cult classics. (p125)

Balboa Theatre Art-deco cinema features first-run and art-house films, plus family matinees. (p157)

Sports

San Francisco 49ers The 49ers were the National Football League dream team during the 1980s to '90s, claiming five Superbowl championships. After decades of chilly, fumbled games at SF's foggy Candlestick Park, the 49ers moved to Santa Clara's brand-new Levi's Stadium in 2014. Some fans argue

EZRA SHAW / GETTY IMAGES ©

the team should be renamed, since Santa Clara's 38 miles from San Francisco. But it was a winning move: Levi's Stadium is hosting Superbowl 50 in 2016. To reach the stadium, take Caltrain one hour south to Santa Clara station, then catch the game-day shuttle.

San Francisco Giants SF's Major League Baseball team is on a World Series winning streak, with beards and women's underwear for luck. (p92)

Golden State Warriors The Bay Area's NBA team plays basketball to win, and took the championship home to Oakland in 2015. Pending completion of a new Warriors stadium, they'll be moving back to San Francisco in 2018.

Survival Guide

Survival Guide

Before You Go

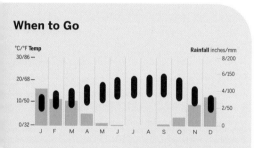

When to Go

°C/°F Temp
30/86 —
20/68 —
10/50 —
0/32 —

Rainfall inches/mm
8/200
6/150
4/100
2/50
0

J F M A M J J A S O N D

➡ **Winter (Dec–Feb)**
Low-season rates, brisk but rarely cold days, and the colorful Lunar New Year parade.

➡ **Spring (Mar–Apr)**
Film festivals, blooming parks and mid-season rates make the occasional damp day worthwhile.

➡ **Summer (May–Aug)**
Street fairs, farmers markets and June Pride celebrations compensate for high-season rates and chilly afternoon fog.

➡ **Fall (Sep–Nov)** Prime time for blue skies, free concerts, better hotel rates and flavor-bursting harvest cuisine.

Book Your Stay

☑ **Top Tip** San Francisco's 16.25% hotel tax is not included in most quoted rates.

➡ Downtown hotels offer bargain rates, but avoid the sketchy, depressing Tenderloin district west of Mason St.

➡ Most motels offer free on-site parking. At downtown hotels, expect to pay $35 to $50 for overnight parking.

Useful Websites

B&B San Francisco
(www.bbsf.com) Personable, privately owned B&Bs and neighborhood inns.

Hotel Tonight (www.hoteltonight.com) SF-based hotel search app offering discount last-minute bookings.

Airbnb (www.airbnb.com) SF-based app offering short-term home-sharing and vacation rentals.

Lonely Planet (www.lonelyplanet.com/usa/san-francisco/hotels) Expert author reviews, user feedback, online bookings.

Best Budget

HI San Francisco Fisherman's Wharf (www.sfhostels.com) Waterfront hostel with million-dollar views.

San Remo Hotel (www.sanremohotel.com) Spartan furnishings, shared bathrooms, great rates.

Pacific Tradewinds Hostel (www.san-francisco-hostel.com) Downtown hostel with snappy design.

Hayes Valley Inn (www.hayesvalleyinn.com) Simple but homey, with shared bathrooms and boutiques at your doorstep.

Coventry Motor Inn (www.coventrymotorinn.com) Value-priced motel with big rooms, free parking and wi-fi.

Marina Inn (www.marinainn.com) Simple, small hotel in prime location near waterfront attractions.

Best Midrange

Hotel Rex (www.jdvhotels.com) Cozy rooms with sumptuous beds and a downstairs literary lounge; off Union Square.

Hotel Bohème (www.hotelboheme.com) North Beach jazz-era gem; small, period-perfect rooms.

Hotel Monaco (www.monaco-sf.com) Snazzy design hotel on an iffy downtown block, with perks aplenty: bikes, wine, gym.

Hotel Carlton (www.jdvhotels.com/hotels/california/san-francisco-hotels/hotel-carlton) Freshly redesigned Nob Hill boutique hotel with good-value rooms.

Hotel Zetta (www.hotelzetta.com) Tech-savvy, artistically inclined hotel in SF's shopping central.

Hotel Del Sol (www.thehoteldelsol.com) Revamped, family-friendly 1950s Marina motel; heated outdoor pool.

Best Top End

Hotel Drisco (www.hoteldrisco.com) Luxury inn atop Pacific Heights.

Loews Regency (www.loewshotels.com/regency-san-francisco) Five-star service; knock-out views.

Palace Hotel (www.sfpalace.com) Stately classical hotel, century-old landmark.

Marker (www.swhotel.com) Snazzy design, useful amenities, central location.

Argonaut Hotel (www.argonauthotel.com) Nautically themed hotel at Fisherman's Wharf.

Arriving in San Francisco

☑ **Top Tip** For the best way to get to your accommodations, see p"Getting Around" on page 17.

From San Francisco International Airport (SFO)

➜ **BART** Direct 30-minute ride to/from downtown San Francisco costs $8.65; SFO BART station is outside the international terminal.

➡ **Door-to-door vans**
Shared vans depart outside baggage claim; 45 minutes to most SF locations; one-way fares $17 to $20. Companies include **SuperShuttle** (☎800-258-3826; www.supershuttle.com), **Quake City** (☎415-255-4899; www.quakecityshuttle.com), **Lorrie's** (☎415-334-9000; www.gosfovan.com) and **American Airporter Shuttle** (☎415-202-0733; www.americanairporter.com).

➡ **Taxis** Depart from outside baggage claim; $40 to $55 to most SF destinations.

➡ **Driving** Downtown San Francisco is a 20- to 60-minute, 14-mile trip north from SFO up Hwy 101.

From Oakland International Airport (OAK)

➡ **BART** BART people-mover shuttles run every 10 to 20 minutes from Terminal 1 to the Coliseum station, where you connect with BART trains to downtown SF ($10.05, 25 minutes).

➡ **Door-to-door vans**
Shared rides to SF run $27 to $35 on **Super-**

Shuttle (☎800-258-3826; www.supershuttle.com).

➡ **Taxis** Depart curbside; fares $60 to $90 to SF.

From Norman Y Mineta San Jose International Airport (SJC)

➡ **Caltrain** The VTA Airport Flyer (bus 10; tickets free, 5am to 11:30pm) departs every 15 to 30 minutes to Santa Clara station, where trains depart to San Francisco. Caltrain terminal is at the corner of 4th and King Sts (one way $9.25, 90 minutes); see www.caltrain.com for details.

➡ **Car** Downtown San Francisco is 50 miles north of SJC, via Hwy 101.

From Emeryville Amtrak Station (EMY)

➡ **Train** Amtrak (☎800-872-7245; www.amtrakcalifornia.com) serves San Francisco via Emeryville (near Oakland), and runs free shuttle buses from its Emeryville station to San Francisco's Ferry Building and Caltrain station.

Getting Around

....

Cable Car

☑ **Best for...** scenic routes and handling hills between downtown and Fisherman's Wharf and North Beach.

➡ **Fares** Tickets cost $7 per ride (no on/off privileges). Purchase on board from conductor or at cable car turnaround kiosks.

➡ **Passes** For multiple rides, get a Muni Passport (one/three/seven days $17/26/35).

➡ **Seating** Each car seats about 30, plus standing passengers clinging to straps. To secure a seat, get on at cable car turnarounds.

Streetcar

☑ **Best for...** travel to the Castro and Ocean Beach and along Market St and the Embarcadero to Fisherman's Wharf.

➡ **Muni streetcar** The N Judah line connects SoMa, downtown and Ocean Beach. The F line connects Fisherman's Wharf to the Castro via the Embarcadero and Market St. The *Muni Street & Transit Map*

is available free online
(www.sfmta.com)

➡ **Tickets** Standard fares
cost $2.25 (exact change
required).

➡ **Schedule** Around 5am
to midnight weekdays;
limited schedules on
weekends. For route-
planning and schedules,
consult http://transit.511.
org; for real-time depar-
tures, see www.nextmuni.
com.

➡ **Night service** L and N
lines operate 24 hours,
but above-ground 'Owl'
buses replace streetcars
between 12:30am and
5:30am.

**Key Routes &
Destinations**

F	Fisherman's Wharf & Embarcadero to Castro
J	Downtown to Mission/ Castro
K, L, M	Downtown to Castro
N	Caltrain and AT&T Park to Haight, Golden Gate Park & Ocean Beach
T	Embarcadero to Caltrain & Bayview

Bus

☑ **Best for...** travel to/
from the Haight, Marina
and the Avenues.

➡ **Muni** SF's bus, streetcar and cable car lines
are operated by **Muni**

(Municipal Transit Agency;
☎511; www.sfmta.com).

➡ **Tickets** Standard fare
$2.25; buy on board
(exact change required)
and at underground Muni
stations. Keep ticket for
transfers (good for 90
minutes on streetcars
and buses), and to avoid
a $100 fine.

➡ **Schedules** On digital
bus-stop displays and
maps, plus http://
transit.511.org; for
real-time departures,
see www.nextmuni.com.
Weekend and evening
service is limited.

➡ **Night service** 'Owl'
service (1am to 5am)
offered on limited lines,
with departures every 30

to 60 minutes; Late Night
Transfers valid for travel
8:30pm to 5:30am.

➡ **System map** Available
free online (www.sfmta.
com).

BART

☑ **Best for...** travel
between downtown and
the Mission, East Bay and
SFO.

➡ **Destinations** Down-
town, Mission District, SF
and Oakland international
airports, Berkeley and
Oakland.

➡ **Schedules** Consult
http://transit.511.org.

➡ **Tickets** Sold in BART
station machines; fares
start at $1.85.

Transit Passes

➡ **Muni Passport** Allows unlimited travel on all
Muni transport, including cable cars; it's sold at
the Muni kiosk at the Powell St cable car turnaround on Market St, San Francisco Visitor Information Center, the TIX Bay Area kiosk at Union
Square and shops around town – see www.sfmta.
com for exact locations. One-day passports can
be purchased from cable car conductors.

➡ **Clipper Cards** Downtown Muni/BART stations
issue the Clipper Card – a reloadable transit card
with a $3 minimum valid for Muni, BART, Caltrain
and Golden Gate Transit (not cable cars). Clipper
cards automatically deduct fares and apply
transfers – only one Muni fare is deducted in a
90-minute period.

Taxi

☑ **Best for...** SoMa and Mission club nights.

➔ **Fares** Meters start at $3.50 plus about $2.75 per mile and 10% tip ($1 minimum).

➔ **Taxi services** Companies with 24-hour dispatches include **DeSoto Cab** (📞 415-970-1300; www.desotogo.com), **Luxor** (📞 415-282-4141; www.luxorcab.com) and **Yellow Cab** (📞 415-333-3333; www.yellowcabsf.com).

Bicycle

☑ **Best for...** sightseeing along the waterfront and west of Van Ness Ave.

Green Tortoise

Green Tortoise (📞 800-867-8647, 415-956-7500; www.greentortoise.com) offers quasi-organized, slow travel on biodiesel-fueled buses with built-in berths from San Francisco to West Coast destinations including Santa Cruz, Death Valley, Big Sur and LA.

➔ **Rentals** Near Golden Gate Park and Fisherman's Wharf.

Car

☑ **Best for...** trips out of town. Avoid driving in San Francisco; traffic is constant, street parking scarce, hills tricky and meter-readers ruthless.

➔ **Garages** Around $2 to $8 per hour ($25 to $50 per day) downtown. For public parking garages, see www.sfmta.com; for a map of garages and rates, see http://sfpark.org. Ask hotels, restaurants and entertainment venues about validation.

➔ **Rentals** Start at $55 per day, $175 to $300 per week, plus 8.75% sales tax and insurance.

➔ **Car share** Prius Hybrids and Minis are rented by the hour with **Zipcar** (📞 866-494-7227; www.zipcar.com) for flat rates (including gas and insurance) starting at $8.25 per hour ($89 per day); $25 application fee and $50 prepaid usage required in advance.

➔ **Rush hour** Avoid peak traffic weekdays (7:30am to 9:30am and 4:30pm to 6:30pm); call 📞 511 for traffic updates.

➔ **Towed cars** Retrieve cars towed for parking violations at **Autoreturn** (📞 415-865-8200; www.autoreturn.com; 450 7th St, SoMa; ⏰ 24hr; Ⓜ 27, 42); fines run $73 plus towing and storage fee, starting at $483.75 for the first four hours.

➔ **Roadside assistance** Members of the **American Automobile Association** (AAA; 📞 800-222-4357, 415-773-1900; www.aaa.com; 160 Sutter St; ⏰ 8:30am-5:30pm Mon-Fri) can call the 📞 800 number anytime for emergency road service and towing.

Parking Restrictions

Red	no parking/stopping
Blue	disabled only
Green	10min 9am-6pm
White	pick-up/drop-off only
Yellow	loading zone 7am-6pm

Essential Information

Business Hours

Nonstandard hours are listed in reviews; standard business hours are as follows:

Banks 9am to 4:30pm or 5pm Monday to Friday (occasionally 9am to noon Saturday)

Offices 8:30am to 5:30pm Monday to Friday

Restaurants Breakfast 8am to 11am, lunch noon to 3pm, dinner 5:30pm with last service 9pm to 9:30pm weekdays or 10pm weekends; Saturday and Sunday brunch 10am to 2pm

Shops 10am to 6pm or 7pm Monday to Saturday, though hours often run 11am to 8pm Saturday, and 11am to 6pm Sunday

Discount Cards

➡ **Go Card** (www.smart-destinations.com; adult/child one day $60/45, two days $88/60, three days $109/80) offers access to major San Francisco attractions and discounts on packaged tours; good value for manic travelers.

➡ **City Pass** (www.citypass.com; adult/child $94/69) covers Muni and cable cars plus four attractions, including California Academy of Sciences, Blue & Gold Fleet Bay Cruise, Aquarium of the Bay and either the Exploratorium or the de Young Museum.

Electricity

120V/60Hz

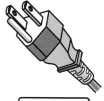

120V/60Hz

Emergency

➡ **Police, fire & ambulance** 🎧emergencies 911, 🎧nonemergencies 311

➡ **San Francisco General Hospital** (🎧emergency 415-206-8111, main hospital 415-206-8000; www.sfdph.org; 1001 Potrero Ave; ⏰24hr; 🚌9, 10, 33, 48)

➡ **Drug & alcohol emergency treatment** 🎧415-362-3400

➡ **Trauma Recovery & Rape Treatment Center** (🎧24hr hotline 415-206-8125, business hours 415-437-3000; www.traumarecovery center.org)

Money

☑ **Top Tip** Most banks have ATMs open 24 hours; service charges may apply.

➡ The US dollar is the only currency accepted in San Francisco; debit/credit cards are accepted widely.

Changing Money

➡ **Exchange bureaus** Located at airports, but most city banks offer better rates – try centrally located **Bank of America** (🎧415-837-1394; www.bankamerica.com; 1 Powell St;

Money-Saving Tips

➜ Summer festivals in Golden Gate Park and neighborhood street fairs are often free.

➜ One day each month is usually free at SF museums, and some evening events offer steeply discounted admission; see individual listings.

➜ Hang on to your Muni ticket for discounted admission at key attractions, including California Academy of Sciences, de Young Museum and Legion of Honor.

🕘9am-6pm Mon-Fri, to 2pm Sat; M Powell, B Powell).

➜ **Exchange rates** Consult www.xe.com, a currency converter site.

Credit Cards & Travelers Checks

Some establishments will accept travelers checks just like cash.

To report lost or stolen credit cards or travelers checks, contact the following numbers:

➜ **American Express** 📞415-536-2600

➜ **Diners Club** 📞800-234-6377

➜ **Discover** 📞800-347-2683

➜ **MasterCard** 📞800-622-7747

➜ **Thomas Cook** 📞800-223-7373

➜ **Visa** 📞800-227-6811

Public Holidays

Holidays that may affect business hours and transit schedules include the following:

New Year's Day January 1

Martin Luther King Jr Day Third Monday in January

Presidents' Day Third Monday in February

Easter Sunday (and Good Friday and Easter Monday) March or April

Memorial Day Last Monday in May

Independence Day July 4

Labor Day First Monday in September

Columbus Day Second Monday in October

Veterans Day November 11

Thanksgiving Fourth Thursday in November

Christmas Day December 25

Safe Travel

☑ **Top Tip** Keep your city smarts and wits about you, especially at night in the Tenderloin, SoMa and the Mission.

➜ After dark, Dolores Park, Buena Vista Park and the entry to Golden Gate Park at Haight and Stanyan Sts can turn seedy with petty drug dealing.

➜ Panhandlers and homeless people are part of San Francisco's urban landscape. People will probably ask you for spare change, but donations to local nonprofits stretch further. For safety, don't engage with panhandlers at night or around ATMs. Otherwise, a simple 'I'm sorry' is a polite response.

Telephone

☑ **Top Tip** North American travelers can use their cell phones in San Francisco and the Bay Area, but should check with their carriers about roaming charges.

➡ **US country code** ☑1

➡ **San Francisco area code** ☑(1) 415

➡ **International calls** From the Bay Area, call ☑011 + country code + area code + number; when calling Canada, skip the initial 011.

➡ **Calling other area codes** The area code must be preceded by a 1.

Area Codes in the Bay Area

➡ **East Bay** ☑510

➡ **Marin County** ☑415

➡ **Peninsula** ☑650

➡ **San Jose** ☑408

➡ **Santa Cruz** ☑831

➡ **Wine Country** ☑707

Cell Phones

➡ Most US cell phones – aside from iPhones – operate on CDMA, not the European standard GSM. Be sure to check compatibility with your phone service provider.

Operator Services

➡ **International operator** ☑00

➡ **Local directory** ☑411

➡ **Long-distance directory information** ☑1 + area code + 555-1212

➡ **Operator** ☑0

➡ **Toll-free number information** ☑800-555-1212

Toilets

☑ **Top Tip** Haight-Ashbury and the Mission District don't have many public toilets – you may have to buy coffee to access locked customer-only bathrooms.

Citywide Self-cleaning, coin-operated outdoor kiosk commodes cost 25¢; there are 25 citywide, mostly located in North Beach, Fisherman's Wharf and downtown. Toilet paper isn't always available.

Downtown Clean toilets and baby-changing tables can be found in **Westfield San Francisco Centre** (www.westfield.com/sanfrancisco; 865 Market St; ⏰10am-8:30pm Mon-Sat, 11am-7pm Sun; 🛗; 🚋Powell-Mason, Powell-Hyde, Ⓜ Powell, Ⓑ Powell).

Civic Center Restrooms are available in **San Francisco Main Library** (☑415-557-4400; www.sfpl.org; 100 Larkin St; ⏰10am-6pm Mon & Sat, 9am-8pm Tue-Thu, noon-6pm Fri, noon-5pm Sun; 📶🛗; 🚌5, 6, 7, 19, 21, 31, Ⓜ Civic Center,

Ⓑ Civic Center), as well as in public library branches and parks throughout the city.

Tourist Information

San Francisco Visitors Information Center (☑415-391-2000; www.sanfrancisco.travel; Hallidie Plaza, Market & Powell Sts, lower level; ⏰9am-5pm Mon-Fri, to 3pm Sat & Sun; 🚋Powell-Mason, Powell-Hyde, Ⓜ Powell St, Ⓑ Powell St) Maps, Muni passports and help with accommodations.

Golden Gate National Recreation Area Headquarters (GGNRA; ☑415-561-4700; www.nps.gov/goga; 495 Jefferson St; ⏰8:30am-4:30pm Mon-Fri; 🚌19, 30, 47, 🚋Powell-Hyde, Ⓜ F) Find everything hikers need to know about the GGNRA, plus maps and information on camping, hiking and programs at these andother national parks in the Pacific West region (including Yosemite).

Travelers with Disabilities

☑ **Top Tip** All Bay Area transit companies offer travel discounts for disabled travelers and wheelchair-accessible service.

Dos & Don'ts

Fashion Casual is the norm, but pretty much anything goes fashion-wise in San Francisco, from bird costumes to glitter thongs. But there is one rule: don't stare.

Food Vegans, pescatarians and allergies are accommodated at many restaurants – but confirm when you call for reservations so the chef can adjust recipes and use separate utensils as needed. Don't be shy about asking about food sourcing – many SF restaurants are proud to serve local, organic, humane, sustainable fare.

Politics Leftist politics are mainstream in San Francisco, as is friendly debate. Don't be shy about sharing your views, and do hear out others.

➡ **Transit** For services, see **San Francisco Bay Area Regional Transit Guide** (www.transit.511.org/disabled/index.aspx).

➡ **Pedestrian crossings** Major downtown crosswalks emit a chirping signal to indicate when it is safe for visually impaired pedestrians to cross the street.

➡ **Wheelchair accessibility** The **Independent Living Resource Center of San Francisco** (📞415-543-6222; www.ilrcsf.org; 🕙9am-4:30pm Mon-Thu, to 4pm Fri) covers Bay Area public transit, hotels and other facilities.

Visas

☑ **Top Tip** Check the **US Department of State** (http://travel.state.gov/content/visas/english/visit/visa-waiver-program.html) for updates and details on the following requirements.

➡ **Canadians** Proof of identity and citizenship required.

➡ **Visa Waiver Program** The VWP allows nationals from 38 countries to enter the US without a visa. It requires a machine-readable passport issued after November 2006.

➡ **Visa required** For anyone staying longer than 90 days, or with plans to work or study in the US.

Behind the Scenes

Send Us Your Feedback

We love to hear from travelers – your comments help make our books better. We read every word, and we guarantee that your feedback goes straight to the authors. Visit **lonelyplanet.com/contact** to submit your updates and suggestions.

Note: We may edit, reproduce and incorporate your comments in Lonely Planet products such as guidebooks, websites and digital products, so let us know if you don't want your comments reproduced or your name acknowledged. For a copy of our privacy policy visit lonelyplanet.com/privacy.

Our Readers

Many thanks to Anthony Oertel and Jacqueline How, who used the last edition and wrote to us with helpful hints, useful advice and interesting anecdotes.

Alison's Thanks

Thanks to Cliff Wilkinson, Alison Ridgway, Sarah Sung, Lisa Park, DeeAnn Budney, PT Tenenbaum, and above all, Marco

Flavio Marinucci, for making a Muni bus ride into the adventure of a lifetime.

Acknowledgements

Cover photograph: Cable car, Massimo Ripani/4Corners ©.

This Book

This fifth edition of Lonely Planet's *Pocket San Francisco* guidebook was coordinated by Alison Bing, and researched and written by Alison Bing and John A Vlahides. The previous edition was also written by Alison Bing. This guidebook was produced by the following:

Destination Editor Clifton Wilkinson

Product Editors Joel Cotterell, Alison Ridgway

Regional Senior Cartographer Alison Lyall

Cartographer Julie Sheridan

Book Designer Michael Buick

Assisting Editors Gabrielle Innes, Kristin Odijk

Cover Researcher Campbell McKenzie

Thanks to Carolyn Boicos, Grace Dobell, Andi Jones, Anne Mason, Catherine Naghten, Claire Naylor, Karyn Noble, Susan Paterson, Angela Tinson, Lauren Wellicome, Tony Wheeler

Index

See also separate subindexes for:

Eating p196

Drinking p197

Entertainment p198

Shopping p198

Sights 000
Map Pages **000**

🍸 Drinking

Our Writer

Alison Bing

Alison has done most things travelers are supposed to do and many you definitely shouldn't, including making room for the chickens, accepting dinner invitations from cults, and trusting the camel to know the way. She has survived to tell tales for Lonely Planet, NPR, BBC Travel, *The Telegraph, New York Times* and other global media.

Contributing Writer

John A Vlahides contributed to Golden Gate Bridge & the Marina and Fisherman's Wharf & the Piers.

Published by Lonely Planet Publications Pty Ltd
ABN 36 005 607 983
5th edition – February 2016
ISBN 978 1 743218587
© Lonely Planet 2016 Photographs © as indicated 2016
10 9 8 7 6 5 4 3 2 1
Printed in China